A
Corpsman's
Legacy

Killed In Action, Corpsman Gary Young
Continues To Heal Others Through The
Daughter He Never Knew

By

Stephanie Hanson Caisse

ACKNOWLEDGMENTS

During my journey recorded in this book, more people helped me than I could ever name. The number of responses I received from strangers answering my request for help was astonishing. I received literally thousands of emails, letter and phone calls. I want to thank each and every person that took the time to write or call me.

The support of my friends and family has been extraordinary, to say the least, and I would never have been able to accomplish what I have done without them. I'm too afraid to try to list them out for fear of accidentally forgetting someone. But you know who you are and how grateful I am to you for standing by my side during this adventure.

I must give special thanks to two people, however.

First, to my beautiful stepdaughter Nikki. Thank you for letting me be the best stepmonster I can be.

And last, but never least... thanks to my husband. I never thought I would marry a Marine, let alone a Purple Fox. And in my wildest dreams, I couldn't have imagined someone would stand by me and be so proud of every step I take. You were more than worth the wait. Rick, you are my love, my hero, my everything.

DEDICATION

To my father,
Gary Norman Young

and the men that were with him
on February 7, 1969

Ernie Bartolina
Russ Moke
Chuck Miller
Rodney Shank (Ronnie Gordon)
Rip Tyrrell
Greg Tomaro

PROLOGUE

IT IS KNOWN TO MANY AS JUST THE WALL. IN THE shadow of the Lincoln Memorial, this slab of black granite appears to emerge right out of the earth. Since its construction in 1982, the Vietnam Veterans Memorial has become one of the most-visited sites in the city of Washington. Although no one is buried at the memorial, it is hallowed ground. Dedicated not only to the 58,249 men and women who made the ultimate sacrifice, it is actually for all those who served in the war, living or dead.

The magic of The Wall has prompted many to call it a place of healing for those affected by one of the most divisive wars in our nation's history. And on my first visit to The Wall, I became one of those believers.

It was a crisp, fall day as I stood in front of the endless list of names etched into the marble. In its mirror-like surface, I could see my own reflection, as well as those of the crowds around me. Grizzled veterans stood and talked to names on The Wall, as I would an old friend, while rivulets of tears streamed down their faces. Women ran their fingers across the engravings, as if touching a name would bring the person back to them. Children stared, not quite comprehending the meaning behind all the names, or the emotions the adults were showing, although they somehow seemed to understand the heartache. But the thousands of names were a mystery to me, as was the war itself.

As I walked further down the path, all of a sudden, I was overcome by an eerie feeling that my birth father's name was on this Wall. I tried to shake the feeling off as foolishness, but it didn't go away.

Factually I knew nothing about my birth father, not his name, or who he was. But even though it didn't seem possible, somewhere deep inside of me, I knew he had died in the Vietnam War.

At that moment, I unwittingly began a journey, although I would not know it for many years to come. Looking at the thousands of names listed, I wondered which one was my father's name? Which one belonged to me?

February 1969 – Vietnam

Marble Mountain Marine Corps Air Facility was a helicopter base built alongside a beautiful beach. The South China Sea extended beyond that beach all the way east to home, the United States, and family and friends. Marble, as affectionately called, was quite a modern base, especially when compared to other bases throughout Vietnam. Dotting the sand not far from the water, dozens of buildings, or hootches, filled the area. These wood and screen-wire structures, topped by corrugated tin roofs, housed Marine Aircraft Group Sixteen, MAG-16 for short, one of the elite helicopter and fixed-wing Air Groups in the Marine Corps.

Standing in the twilight outside his hootch, a soft

breeze whisked away the smoke from his cigarette as Gary Young thought of what lay ahead tomorrow when he would fly for the first time. Far away he heard the sound of artillery booming like an incessant thunderstorm. As far as one could see, parachute flares lit up the night sky. Off in the distance, outlined by the eerie glow of the descending flares, Gary looked at the monolith from which the base got its name – Marble Mountain. The steel-gray mass of jagged rock was the only high ground in any direction. Dozens of red tracer rounds from automatic weapons fired towards the mountain following the distinctive sound of the enemy's AK-47 assault rifle. Gary knew somewhere out there Marines dueled with the enemy. He pulled deeply on his cigarette, then exhaled and wondered if those Marines fighting out there might be his first patients.

His thoughts were a jumble. *What will tomorrow be like? I'm pretty sure I'm ready, but how can I know?* He had the best training to be a corpsman, but this was different. He would care for patients inside a trembling, bucking, roaring helicopter, perhaps under fire. He completed his ground orientation. He climbed all over the airplane, called "the bird" in Navy-Marine Corps idiom, parts explained, the routines demonstrated. He knew about the fifty-caliber machine guns mounted on the left and right behind the cockpit. The gunners and the crew chief owned those, but in the rear back by the big open door, its access ramp and beneath the engines he had his domain. A couple of green canvas litters, stained brown with old blood, and boxes of bottles of intravenous fluid positioned for whoever walked, crawled or was carried up the ramp. He drew some comfort knowing tomorrow Walter "Rip" Tyrrell, another corpsman, would fly with him. Rip would make sure he didn't stray or would extend his steady hand if things got too hectic.

Gary laughed to himself when he thought of the good-natured hazing he received since reporting to Marble. As the FNG, the "Fucking New Guy," he had been "in-country" for a little over four months, but assigned to a dispensary supporting jets. When he volunteered to transfer to MAG-16 to fly, the guys laughed at him.

"You *asked* to fly?"

"You *like* being surrounded by jarheads all day?"

"You *want* to get your ass shot off?"

But the teasing didn't deter his desire to fly medevacs. Gary knew medevac birds landed where the action is, swooping in to gather up wounded Marines and take them as fast as they can to the medical facilities in the rear. Where there are wounded, there are enemy soldiers who would like nothing more than to knock a helicopter out of the sky. Waiting back at the dispensary for the injuries to come in frustrated him to the point of volunteering. Perhaps being in the field would allow him the few precious seconds sometimes needed to help save more lives.

As soon as Gary arrived at MAG-16, he heard about the medevac bird that went down recently, its crew, including a corpsman, lost. Part of his FNG welcome included teasing about this event.

"Hey, FNG, this will be your fate too. You had better get right with the world!"

Gary smiled and replied, "Never happen!"

He finished his cigarette and flicked the butt into the sand. He looked across the street at the lights in the clinic, the MAG-16 dispensary, where he worked since reporting to Marble a few days ago. Its little cluster of buildings, built of the same materials as the hootches, housed the treatment rooms, x-ray machine, lab and pharmacy that provided the daily care needed by a busy air facility. Its twenty or so corpsmen and half-dozen physicians provided the staff for the medevac missions as well.

He turned toward his hootch and thought, *how boring the mélange of maladies treated at daily sick call and how exciting it will be to fly.* He shivered a little and opened the door. "Damn, this is going to be fun."

Minutes later he scrounged up a piece of paper to pen a letter to send to a high-school buddy.

I've finally been transferred to MAG-16. I will be flying on choppers. I fly my first medevac mission tomorrow. I'm going to put a big sign on the bird that says "Do Not Shoot." Hope it works. HA!!

Gary finished his note when Bill Sperb, another corpsman, walked in.

"What'cha doing?" Bill asked.

"Writing everyone back home, making sure they have my new address," Gary replied.

"Don't forget to warn all the girls we are going to tear up the town together when we get home."

Gary once again silently marveled at the fates that brought him halfway around the world and stationed him with a corpsman from Sandy, a suburb of his hometown of Portland, Oregon. Although they hadn't known each other back home, they had become fast friends in Vietnam.

"Hah! You're so ugly, I'll be the one getting all the girls," Gary retorted good-naturedly.

In truth, Bill could probably get any girl he wanted with his handsome looks, his blond hair that flopped over his eyes and his charming smile. Bill, however, didn't have a lot on Gary in the looks department. Gary's sandy hair, green eyes and crooked grin attracted more than a fair share of the ladies.

"You fly tomorrow, don't you? Got all your gear?" Bill asked.

Gary nodded. The flight gear he had been issued amazed him, especially the strangest device of body armor, called a "bullet bouncer." Similar to equipment worn by bomber crews in World War II and constructed of ceramic material, its front and back plates together weighed a whopping 49 pounds. The two plates, worn like a vest, could stop shrapnel or small bullets, but its weight and the heat it trapped, made it onerous. The body armor ensemble also included a crotch protector that looked like overgrown jockey shorts. Nobody wore those. The second-hand flight helmet, refurbished but still smelling of someone else's sweat, weighed three pounds all by itself. Its two sliding plastic faceplates, one tinted for sun protection and the other clear, did little to keep dust and debris out of the eyes. The green flight suit was made of Nomex, a fire-resistant material that provided a few seconds of protection if one needed to escape a burning wreck. The issued flight gloves of Nomex and leather seemed useless to corpsmen, since he couldn't check a pulse or clamp a pulsing artery wearing gloves. Rounding out the equipment was a shoulder holster and a .38 revolver for personal protection and to defend the patient, although it was a weapon acknowledged by everyone to be useless.

"I can't believe how much this stuff weighs," remarked Gary.

"Believe me, when the bullets start flying and you're ankle deep in blood, you won't notice the weight," Bill replied. "I hear Rip is showing you the ropes."

Gary nodded in the affirmative. He thought about Rip and his expectations and hoped he wouldn't disappoint. The other corpsmen told him repeatedly that no matter how well-trained and how experienced, when you tended the wounded in a vibrating helicopter, often under fire, everything was different.

Bill left the hootch and left Gary to his letter writing.

MARINE MEDEVAC HELICOPTERS ARE NOT THE speedy little single-rotor birds with the big red crosses painted on their sides favored by the Army. The Marines used the big CH-46 Sea Knight transport helicopters with the double rotors. The "forty-six," termed by those who rode or depended upon them, could transport a heavy load but were vulnerable. Many were lost when small arms fire took out the airplane's hydraulic boost – its power steering. The Marine Corps simply could not afford a separate fleet of medical evacuation helicopters, so it used its transport fleet. Instead of red crosses the helicopters had machine guns, although the consensus among those who flew medevacs in Vietnam was that the red crosses mattered little. The enemy used the crosses as targets most of the time.

The Marines depend upon the Navy to provide their corpsmen. The Marine Corps corpsman is a Sailor dressed like a Marine and only gets a month of combat training. The attrition rate in combat is very high. The Marines know corpsmen don't have combat training equivalent to themselves and try to take care of their "docs." Their lives, literally, depend on it. The enemy can always tell who the corpsmen are, as they rush around saving lives. In Vietnam, the enemy did not respect the Geneva Convention, among which are the articles providing protection for medical personnel in combat.

Gary, like most corpsmen, considered the saving of lives to be paramount. To someone outside the medical community, this might seem a little strange. Why would a young person volunteer to place himself in danger and to deal daily with the broken and bleeding? There is no answer. They just do. Gary, proud of his choice, felt the medevac corpsman was the pinnacle. He would be proud to earn the wings signifying his accomplishment.

In the hot mugginess, Gary awakened early, clad in a towel and shod in flip-flops, he went across the street for his shower. Corpsmen had it better than the Marines, for they had hot water. An outdoor shower next to the operating room hootch sported a hot-water heater. The Marines wanted their corpsmen clean and provided accordingly. It really didn't matter; since the effects of the shower didn't last long anyway.

He put on his green flight suit and wandered over to the dispensary. Breakfast consisted of a couple of cups of awful sickbay coffee left in the pot by the night crew. Coffee and a few cigarettes, he figured, were about all his butterfly-ridden stomach could tolerate.

Gary saw Rip approach and he grabbed his gear for the drive to the flight line by one of their senior corpsmen, Bill Dial. Dial helped him throw his gear into the back of the jeep ambulance along with Rip's. Gary felt better just being with Rip; besides him being a plain nice guy with a lot of confidence, he had the experience of thirteen months in Vietnam.

"You all set?" Rip asked. "Let's do it. It ain't gonna get any better," he teased in a way that made Gary laugh.

"See you tonight," someone else said. No hoopla. No sendoff. Just another day of business hunting Charlie.

"Ready?" Dial asked.

The trip to the flight line didn't take long, but to Gary it seemed to go in slow motion. He thought, *what if I forget something? What if I completely fuck up? People's lives will depend on me now more than ever. What if I can't handle it?*

As if he could read Gary's mind, Rip reached over and gave him a reassuring slap on the back. His look seemed to say, "It will be okay."

They pulled up to the helicopters assigned to fly the medevac mission. Gary and Rip would fly with Marine Medium Helicopter Squadron HMM-364, nicknamed the "Purple Foxes." The pilots and crew, busy readying the aircraft, took a moment to greet the corpsmen.

"Nice to meet'cha, Doc," the Marines said in unison.

Although Gary had been called "Doc" a thousand times by now, he still felt pride when one of his Marines called him that. He thought how funny it was that one small word could infer so much honor and dignity.

Medevac birds flew in pairs. The lead bird, the first of the pair, carried the corpsmen. The second bird, called the chase, was there in case the lead bird had problems. The lead helicopter's radio call sign would technically be "Swift 1-1," but the dispatchers and everyone else called it "Swift Medevac." The chase's call sign would be "Swift 1-2."

Rip showed Gary the helicopter in which they would fly then arranged the equipment and supplies they would need. Bandages of various size and type were in greatest demand. Rip showed Gary how to stuff the many pockets of his flight suit with bandages and dressings to make the supplies readily available when needed most. Corpsmen carried homemade kits for opening the throats of patients who could not breathe because of injuries to the face or neck. Rip showed his to Gary and said he would help him make one of his own. He connected Gary's helmet to the aircraft intercom system, which would allow him to hear the pilots and other crewmembers as the mission progressed. Most flights, after the patients got on board, only lasted about fifteen to twenty minutes.

The crew chief came back to the rear of the bird and handed each a small stack of business cards.

"The Foxes like us to give these to anyone we transport," Rip explained. "Even if we just tuck them in a patient's pocket."

Gary looked at one of the cards. On it was the cartoon logo of the Purple Fox and the words, "This trip courtesy of the Purple Foxes. Give a shit." The crew wanted the troops they carried to know that somebody cared about them, that they did "give a shit."

Gary chuckled. This fit perfectly with the Purple Fox reputation.

Before long, Gary noticed the co-pilot on the left side of the cockpit busily writing on his kneeboard, a small clipboard strapped to his upper leg. The pilot on the other side of the cockpit looked at a map.

"We've got a mission," Rip said.

The crew chief began the startup procedures and the big rotors started to turn.

Gary looked out the windows on the gunner's side and saw the ground getting farther away. *Finally now I'm a flying doc, the ultimate experience for a corpsman. I'll have my wings in no time.*

BUSINESS AT MARBLE CONTINUED AS USUAL. Helicopters and fixed-wing aircraft came and went while ground personnel worked on birds scheduled for maintenance. At sickbay, morning sick call was underway. Corpsmen from the dispensary were at the mess hall doing sanitation inspections.

Several hours later, a call came into the squadron operations center. The HMM-364 duty officer listened intently and then grabbed his messenger, a young enlisted Marine, and issued terse instructions. The messenger ran off to alert the head of the recovery team.

The messenger gasped, "Sir, Swift Medevac is down. Swift 1-1 is down in the zone. No activity noted..."

ONE

THERE ARE MANY DIFFERENT MOMENTS I COULD point to and say where my story really began. The day my parents told me I was adopted – although to be honest, I was so young, I can't say I actually remember it. Or the day my doctor diagnosed me with Multiple Sclerosis. Perhaps when I found out my birth mother was not dead as I thought, but alive. In hindsight, my journey seems to have started on my first trip to The Wall. But the moment I realized nothing in my life was going to be the same again, was the day I first met my birth mother.

It was supposed to be just one simple meeting. A couple of hours to get medical questions answered, and then my life could go on as usual. Little did I know how this one meeting would trigger a chain of events that would change not only my life, but the lives of countless others.

In all of my twenty-six years of life, I had never given the notion of finding my birth parents more than a fleeting thought. As I sat in my aunt's kitchen waiting for my birth mother to arrive, I realized I still hadn't recovered from the shock of the events of the past four weeks.

I had been quite sick for the past several months and a little over a month ago, my doctor finally diagnosed me with Multiple Sclerosis and desperately wanted me to find out my medical history. My parents, Dale and Gabriella Hanson, adopted me at birth through an anonymous adoption. My adoptive parents had never known about my biological parents, although through the hospital grapevine, they heard my birth mother died several years after my adoption. So when we contacted the hospital, they told us the only way they would release my medical records was for us to produce my birth mother's signature or her death certificate.

My dad ended up discovering a group called the Oregon Adoption Rights Association. He and I attended one of their monthly meetings, where we were introduced to their self-appointed sleuth named Mary. She was quite successful in tracking down birth parents, and we hoped she could use her talents to dig up a death certificate on my birth mother. We gave her what little details we had and left, feeling somewhat pessimistic about our chances of ever getting the information I needed.

But the very next morning, Mary called me at work. I couldn't understand why she would call so soon, but the tone of her voice when she asked if I was sitting down, made me sink quietly into my chair.

"Yes, I am," I replied cautiously. "What is it?"

"I've discovered the identity of your birth mother," Mary said. "She's not dead like you thought. Her name is Linda and she lives less than fifteen miles from you."

At Mary's suggestion, my aunt Carol made the initial contact with her. How she would react was unpredictable and having an intermediary seemed like the best situation. But even with my aunt contacting her

2

first, getting my birth mother to agree to a meeting proved difficult. The only reason she reluctantly agreed was because of my medical situation. She made it very clear this would be the one and only meeting. In fact, she cancelled the first meeting and I feared she might not show today. Part of me didn't want to meet her, although I knew that doing so would allow me to move on to dealing with my Multiple Sclerosis diagnosis. But faced with such an unfriendly reception, all I wanted was to get this meeting over with. Now, I sit here about to come face-to-face with my birth mother for the first time in my life.

Not long after I arrived, Carol looked out the kitchen window. "Her car is pulling into the driveway."

Not wanting Linda to feel like I would attack her the minute she walked in the door, I went into the living room and sat down. The door opened and I heard Linda walk in the house and greet my aunt. I listened to her footsteps come closer and anxiously watched the doorway. I couldn't quite grasp the fact that within seconds I would see my birth mother for the first time. I wondered if I would see myself in her, or just a faint resemblance. Then Linda walked into the living room and it startled me to see my own brown hair, brown eyes and straight nose on this woman. We were even almost the same height with the same petite figure. It felt surreal to look at a person, a complete stranger, and yet so familiar all at the same time.

Carol made formal, although unnecessary introductions, and then left the room for us to have a private conversation. Linda sat down on the couch opposite me, but for a moment we didn't talk. I recognized the look on her face as one I had used myself. It said *I don't want to be here, but I feel it's my duty.* It appeared I would have to start the conversation, so I decided to focus on medical questions, rather than personal ones.

"I guess the main reason for us meeting is for me to find out if there is any medical history I should know about," I said.

"No, there isn't," Linda quickly replied. "Actually, I don't know much about my own history. The only part I know is my mother's side. I don't really know anything about my father's. And I don't know anything about your father's family history."

That was it. One-fourth of my medical history. I had been so sure my medical questions would be answered today, but I was no better off now than before.

Confused at this turn of events, I sat in silence. The mention of my birth father seemed to hang in the air. When it didn't look like she would elaborate any further on him, I decided I had the right to ask.

"Who is my father?"

Linda looked at me for a while. I could tell she didn't want to answer my question. "Your father was killed in Vietnam," she finally said quietly.

At these words, the hairs on the back of my neck stood on end. Over the past four years the certainty my father was on the Vietnam Memorial Wall had faded. But now, here was proof I *had* been right all those years before. Part of me accepted this acknowledgement calmly, yet another part felt dazed at this revelation.

"What was his name?" I eventually asked.

She hesitated and again it didn't appear she would answer me.

"I only ask because I lived in Washington D.C. for several years and visited The Wall. I don't want to cause any problems, it would just be nice look up his name the next time I am there," I said.

Finally she replied, "His name was Gary Young."

I let that sink in for a minute and then realized since she answered the medical questions and identified my birth father, I didn't really know what else to talk about. And it appeared obvious Linda felt more and more uncomfortable as time went on.

I thought, to hell with it. I don't need to learn any more, and even if she didn't want to talk about her life, I had nothing to hide. So I started to talk about various inane things, such as the weather or the song playing on the radio in the background. Finally she warmed up a bit when she saw I wasn't going to pry any further into her personal life.

"Carol told me you know about my other daughter, Cindy. She is only a couple of years younger than you. But I don't think you know about my son, John, a senior in high school."

Mary discovered the birth certificate on my half-sister, but she hadn't found anything regarding a half-brother. However before we had a chance to talk about it anymore, Linda looked at her watch and said she had to leave to pick up John.

She gathered her things and then stopped for a moment. "Carol told me you are having an MRI soon. I would really like to know the results of it, if you don't mind," she said kindly.

"Of course not. Would it be easier on everyone if I had Carol call you when I find out?" I asked, pleased at the interest. "I really don't want to be intrusive."

She thought about it and after a moment agreed. I believe this finally convinced her I wasn't going to force myself into her life.

She stood up and I knew our conversation ended. We

said good-bye awkwardly; although usually a moment for hugs, this meeting did not lend itself to that type of intimacy. I walked with her into the kitchen where she said good-bye to Carol. When she closed the door, I wondered if I would ever see or talk to her again.

Carol watched Linda through the window and after a few seconds exclaimed, "She's coming back!"

Linda walked back in the door and I could see tears on her face. Coming up to me, she threw her arms around me in a hug. She stated between sobs, "I can't turn my back on you any more than I could on Cindy or John. You remind me so much of them. You *are* my daughter."

After we hugged and cried for a few minutes, Linda said she really did have to leave.

"I can't offer any promises at this time. I've never told my husband or kids about you and I don't really know if I can do it now. I guess I have a lot of thinking to do," she admitted. "But I promise to keep in touch and be sure to let me know how your tests turn out."

And with that, she left again. Deep down, I realized there was a connection with her, a bond I hadn't thought would exist. I liked her, but wasn't sure what would come of this.

The next morning Carol called. "I just received a very nice phone call from Linda and she would like to speak with you as soon as possible."

Getting Linda's home number from Carol, I quickly placed the call.

As soon as Linda heard my voice she said, "Hi, sweetie."

Those two words filled my heart with joy and I realized I did want us to have a relationship, something I hadn't been ready to admit before.

"Well, things didn't turn out quite as I expected yesterday," she said. "After I got home, I spent the rest of the day trying to think of what I should do. My husband, Mark, noticed how distracted I was and took our son John out to a movie, so I could sort through things. He also noticed I didn't get much sleep at all and called in and took the day off of work. He sat me down and asked what bothered me. As much as I wanted to tell him the truth, I wasn't really sure how to come out and say it. I tried, but kept stumbling over the words. But I guess he figured it out and he just sat back and laughed."

"He laughed?" I asked. "That's not the reaction I would have thought he would have."

"Neither did I," Linda said. "But he said 'Linda, I've known you gave a child up for adoption for over twenty years. You told me before we ever got married!' I guess I must have blocked it out.

"He wants to meet you, honey, but I told him I needed to start over with you first before I introduced you to the rest of the family. Would you like to have dinner with me?" she asked,

"I would love that," I honestly answered.

When we met the next evening, Linda immediately gave me a big hug and I realized how anxious she was for me to like her too.

Linda asked lots of questions, trying to get a feeling for what my life had been like.

"Well, I had a pretty typical childhood, I guess," I said. "I've lived all my life in Portland, except for the years I went to college in Washington, D.C. Two years after my parents adopted me, they adopted my brother, Geoff. He and I are the best of friends, probably due to our parents divorcing when I was eleven and he, nine.

The divorce turned ugly and when Geoff and I went to live with my mom, we learned to depend on each other."

"Does Geoff live here in Portland too?" she asked.

"He does. He joined the Marines after high school where he met his wife, Ann, also a Marine. He was in the Gulf War and when he returned, they moved back to Portland right before I came home from college. In fact, my first nephew, Dylan, was one of the main reasons I returned home," I laughed. "I couldn't stand the thought of my two-year-old nephew not knowing me. And they've just discovered Ann is pregnant again, so this time I'll be there from the beginning."

"Did your parents ever remarry?"

"Yes, my mom remarried just a couple of years after the divorce. My stepfather's name is Tony Finch and they had a daughter when I was in high school. Her name is Ashley. She's fifteen years younger than me, so she is eleven now.

"It took a lot longer for my dad to remarry, but he eventually married Patti before I went to college. She had three children from her previous marriage, so I have two stepsisters and a stepbrother. My family tree is more like a forest," I said ruefully.

We continued to ask and answer questions until Linda pulled a piece of paper out of her purse and slid it across the table to me. I picked it up and noticed it seemed like some sort of program folded in half. When I opened it, a newspaper clipping fell out. Glancing down, I saw the headline "Portland Navyman Killed In Crash Of Helicopter." My heart skipped a beat and I knew immediately it was a newspaper write-up of my birth father's death. But more important than the written words, was the accompanying photograph. The first glimpse of my father shook me to the core. My eyes riveted on the smiling young man and I picked it up to take a closer look. My father had my smile! Or more accurately, I had his crooked grin, the one I always wanted to be different. In that brief moment, I realized I would never want to change it again.

I looked at Linda. "This is my smile."

"Yes, that was one of the first things I noticed. You definitely have Gary's mouth. In fact, you look and act exactly like him, even down to your facial expressions and the way you speak. Would you like to hear a little about him?"

"Absolutely. As much as you feel comfortable talking about."

"Well, we met after high school and dated off and on for a couple of years. Eventually Gary joined the Navy and headed down to San Diego. He came home on leave a few times before he went to Vietnam. Shortly after he left, I discovered I was pregnant. I wasn't sure what to do and kept the news from everyone but my roommate. I avoided all of my friends that knew Gary and didn't tell my family either."

Linda continued, "But eventually I realized Gary had the right to know about his child and tried to decide how to tell him. I didn't want to send that type of news in a letter, so I thought of trying to meet him in Hawaii on his R&R. But, he was killed in early February, a few weeks before this. So I never got to tell him."

"He never knew you were pregnant?" I asked. "Did anyone in his family know?"

"No, I never told anyone. When you were born in April, I put you up for adoption, hoping to give you a better life than I could provide for you as an unmarried and single mom in the 1960s."

In all my thoughts about my birth parents, never once had I imagined my father wouldn't have known about me. Would he have been happy when he found out? Or upset? Sadly, I realized these questions would never get answered.

I sensed Linda was having difficulty in keeping her composure and decided to save other questions for later. She told me the clipping was mine to keep and I put it in my purse, thankful I could read it later in private.

We changed the subject and continued talking until out of the corner of my eye, I saw a man approach our table. He stopped and stood quietly staring at me with a smile. I looked up at him and he just continued to smile. I looked back at Linda and wondered what to do.

"Mark, what are you doing here?" she laughed.

Her husband slid into the booth next to her. "I couldn't wait any longer to meet Stephanie and figured you'd be in one of two restaurants. I took a chance and stopped in here on my way home from work."

It flattered me he was so anxious to meet me. I don't think a lot of people would have been as pleasant in the same situation. When Linda excused herself from the table, I waited until she was out of earshot. "You're sure being a good sport about all of this."

"I accepted Cindy as my daughter, why not you too?" he replied.

"Well, at least it didn't come as a complete surprise to you," I said. "Think of what a shock it would have been if she hadn't told you about me all those years ago."

"Oh, I would have known anyway," Mark laughed.

"How?

"When Linda went in the hospital about to give birth to John, the nurse asked her if this was her first child. Already in labor and not thinking clearly, she replied it was her third time. Cindy made one, John made two, where the heck was the third one? I never told her what she said and I am sure she doesn't remember it either."

We both broke out laughing.

OVER THE NEXT SEVERAL MONTHS WE SPENT quite a lot of time together. Eventually, I met my half-sister and half-brother, as well as other various family members. But the most amazing thing happened after I first met Linda. All my symptoms of Multiple Sclerosis disappeared. In the beginning, we thought it was just temporary, but as time passed, the doctors finally admitted the diagnosis was made in error.

I know had I not been diagnosed with Multiple Sclerosis, I most likely would never have searched out Linda. While the months I had been sick were difficult ones, it was all worth it to discover I had such a wonderful birth mother. For a long time, I believed that God just wanted me to find her, and therefore gave me a tiny nudge.

Little did I know this was just the beginning.

TWO

ONE TINY NEWSPAPER OBITUARY. SOMETIMES IT'S hard to believe it all started with one yellowed piece of paper. Just four little paragraphs.

Portland Navyman Killed In
Crash Of Helicopter

Gary Norman Young, 20, a Portland Navy medic serving in Vietnam with the First Marine Regiment, was killed in action last Friday near An Hoa, according to news received by his family in Portland.

The medic was on an emergency mission to a scene of action seven miles northwest of An Hoa in Quang Nam Province when the helicopter in which he was riding encountered intense small arms and automatic fire and crashed, killing Young.

Young was born in Portland and graduated from Wilson High School. He entered the Navy and received training as a medic after which he was assigned to the First Marines. He is survived by his father, stepfather and brothers.

Funeral arrangements in charge of J.P. Finley & Sons,
have not been announced pending arrival of the body
from Vietnam.

In the program from the funeral service, I found the actual dates of my father's life, born on November 3, 1948, and killed on February 7, 1969, a little over two months before my birth on April 21, 1969. This meant he died shortly after he turned twenty years old. At this point in my life, I already outlived my father by six years.

I was bitterly disappointed by how little information appeared in the newspaper obituary, which actually produced more questions than answers.

I had assumed Gary was killed in a firefight on the ground. So what role did helicopters play in the war? Why was a medic on a helicopter? Was he just a passenger? And what was a Navy medic doing serving with Marines? Where was An Hoa? What was Vietnam all about?

I felt guilty I knew so little about Vietnam. I'm sure I studied it in school, but I could only recall it was the first war the United States had lost and most people didn't like to talk about it.

The one redeeming part of the article was the photograph, which I studied closely. It was uncanny, and even eerie, how much I looked like him. I had gone my whole life never really looking like anyone, and to see my face looking back at me, identical eyes, nose, mouth, ears and even the hairline, seemed quite unnerving.

It's hard, if not impossible, to explain how I felt about my father as I stared at his picture. How I could feel so much sadness for someone I had never known and so bothered by an incident that happened a quarter of a century before. But at that moment, I felt a tug in my heart I never felt before. A familiarity, a certain awareness. It sounds far-fetched, but somewhere deep down inside I knew I was just like him. Unfortunately, this awareness only made me more miserable.

The next day I took the newspaper clipping to show my co-workers. It was great hearing everyone say I looked exactly like my father, but difficult when they had questions I couldn't answer. Once they read the newspaper clipping, they knew as much as I did about him.

Two people at work had different reactions. After reading the clipping, Al Patz said, "You need to talk to Larry Jacob about this."

Larry worked for a manufacturing company that rented space in our building. I had only spoken with him a few times on work-related business and he had the reputation of being stern and a bit aloof.

"Why?" I asked.

"You just need to. He will explain why."

I didn't feel comfortable, but finally relented and went to Larry's office. I handed him the newspaper clipping. "Al wanted you to read this."

Larry read the story silently. When he was finished, he asked, "Who is this story about?"

"My birth father. I was adopted at birth and just found out who he was last night."

"So your dad was a corpsman." He studied my face.

I nodded.

"Do you know what that means?" Larry asked.

"A medical person," I shrugged.

"Your dad was a corpsman and you *don't* know what that means. Let me tell you exactly what kind of man your dad was. I was a jet pilot over in Vietnam. The corpsmen were my heroes. And the medevac corpsmen were the best of the best. I owe my life to a corpsman who saved me when my jet crashed once."

I didn't know how to respond to this. I hadn't quite thought of my father in these terms. Larry could see I didn't really understand and went on to explain further.

"Being a medevac corpsman meant they went into some of the most dangerous parts of combat while rescuing wounded Marines. One of the ways for the corpsmen in Vietnam to get their wounded out of the jungle was to have the helicopter hover as low as the pilot could get it. The corpsman would then be lowered on a cable down into the trees, retrieve the wounded and bring them back up." Larry took a deep breath before continuing. "In situations like this the helicopter and the corpsmen were sitting ducks for the enemy. I was rescued in this manner actually more than once."

I could see the tears in Larry's eyes and he swallowed hard. I wasn't sure how to respond to this kind of emotion and didn't know any appropriate thing to say, so I stood quietly.

"Stephanie, you should be very proud of your father, because he was a great man. Your father was truly a hero."

Larry was the first person to call my father a hero, but he wouldn't be the last.

The second unique reaction came from Maureen Doherty, another co-worker and a good friend of mine.

After she read the clipping, she commented, "So, have you been to his grave yet?"

I laughed, "Mo, I've barely known this information for twelve hours. I haven't had time to even think about going there."

"Well, why don't I go up there with you at lunch?"

After stopping at a florist to pick up flowers, we drove to Finley's cemetery and got instructions of where to go from the main office.

When we got out of the car, Maureen headed in one direction and I went in the other to search for the grave. At first I thought we had been given the wrong location because the dates on all the graves seemed to be very recent. But, finally I noticed older graves mixed in with the newer ones. We searched for quite a while and the longer we searched, the more puzzled I became. It would seem between the two of us, one of us should have located the grave by now.

At last I saw the marker created from a slab of black marble – coincidentally just like The Wall.

Gary Norman Young
1948 – 1969
May we remember he died for peace.

Maureen could tell from the look on my face I had found it, and she walked over and took my hand. We stood silently, neither of us knowing what to say.

After a few long minutes, Maureen asked if I wanted to be alone. When I nodded, she quietly walked back to her car. I kneeled down and gently brushed the stray leaves and grass off the marker set flush in the ground before laying down my yellow roses.

My certainty from the night before began to waver. Was I really like him? Or did I imagine it? What had his life really been like?

Standing in the cold winter sunshine, I realized I wasn't going to find the answers to these questions. I couldn't search out his family after all these years and make them relive Gary's death. I felt there was no way I could justify interrupting their lives and bringing back all the pain of losing Gary, just to answer a few questions of mine. The kinder thing to do would be to leave them alone. Especially since they had no idea I even existed. I could learn to live with the questions.

FOR THE NEXT SEVERAL MONTHS, I IGNORED ALL thoughts of my father. Some times were more difficult than others, but I still believed I made the right decision.

Appropriately enough, Veteran's Day changed my mind. While getting ready for work, *The Today Show* ran a segment on the annual ceremony at the Vietnam Memorial Wall in Washington, D.C. The camera panned over the names engraved on The Wall, and I searched the television screen trying to see Gary's name. Obviously a futile search, given the hundreds of names flashing by, but I couldn't help myself.

Veteran's Day had never really meant anything to me before, other than all the government workers got the day off. But watching the ceremony, I realized the greater significance to this day and I somehow needed to honor it and my father.

The only way I could think to do this was to leave flowers again at my father's grave. I didn't really want to go alone, so I invited Shelly Winter, another friend from work, who I promised to take the next time I went.

The cemetery was crowded when we arrived, but I assumed we must have arrived during a funeral ceremony. Even when I noticed a crowd gathered a few yards above Gary's grave, I didn't give it much thought.

After I laid the flowers on his headstone, I tried to concentrate on thoughts of Gary, but the nearby gathering kept catching my attention. I studied the people closer, and eventually noticed some of those in the crowd were men in full-dress military uniforms. Listening more closely to the main speaker, I realized the ceremony honored veterans who died during their wartime service. Finally the true meaning of Veteran's Day dawned on me. Where some people think to honor the living veterans, those living veterans honor their fallen buddies, like my father. I felt compelled to go talk to some of the veterans, but I had no idea of what to say and again felt ashamed at how little I knew about Vietnam.

And with a great flash of insight, I realized my foolishness. This war changed the course of my life and I needed to know about it and about my father's role in it. Was he proud of what he did in Vietnam? Was he scared in the end? How did he die?

I looked down once more at my father's grave, and vowed to find the answers to my questions.

THIS SEEMED LIKE AN IMPOSSIBLE SEARCH AND I didn't have a clue on how to begin. Suddenly I realized the answer came from my computer at work – the Internet. Although we received access only recently, it was reported to be a fantastic research tool, that is, if I could figure out to use it.

I located a popular search engine and tapped away at my keyboard. Searching for *Vietnam* brought in 56,449 matches. Trying just *corpsman* still got over 500 sites. Maybe this wouldn't be so simple. I spotted an advanced search option, which let you search for two terms at one time. I thought about what I wanted to know and decided to see if I could find any formal records on the incident. Searching for *Vietnam* and *helicopters* gave me more promising results.

The top match showed the *Vietnam Helicopter Flight Crew Network* site. Full of data, I quickly realized I didn't have enough information about Gary to make sense of it all. I didn't even know what unit he had been in, and most of the terminology went over my head.

However, browsing through some of the other sites listed was also discouraging. Frustrated, I went back to the *Vietnam Helicopter Flight Crew Network* site. At the bottom it listed the name and email address of the founder of the group. Did I dare write to him and ask for help? I decided the worst he could do was delete my email, but to my utter surprise, I received a return note within an hour.

To: **Stephanie Hanson**
From: **Mel Canon**
Date: **Tues, Nov 12, 1996 2:24pm**

Hi Stephanie...

Thank you for allowing us to try and help you find information relating to your father. I want to let you know how I am sorry for your loss and I hope we can help you to find some closure on this part of your life.

We have helped several others achieve the same thing and will continue to avail ourselves to that worthy cause. I have ordered a database search to try and find whatever information is available relative to this accident. It should come back to me in a day or so...maybe even sooner.

As soon as I find out anything I will let you know.

Mel Canon
Founder, VHFCN

The kindness Mel showed, especially to a stranger, was unexpected. It helped to know others out there have searched as well.

Another site extremely helpful was *The Vietnam Casualty Search Page*. Its database of all those killed in Vietnam produced a page of information when I input Gary's name, branch of service, hometown and state.

Last name: YOUNG
First name: GARY NORMAN
Home of Record (official): PORTLAND
State (official): OR
Date of Birth: Wednesday, November 3, 1948
Sex: Male
Race: Caucasian
Marital Status: Single

— Military —
Branch: Navy
Rank: HN
Serial Number: B824767
Pay grade: E3
MOS (Military Occupational Specialty code): HN

— Action —
Start of Tour: Tuesday, September 10, 1968
Date of Casualty: Friday, February 7, 1969
Age at time of loss: 20
Casualty type: (A1) Hostile, died

Reason: Air loss - Crashed on land
    (Crew member - Helicopter)
Country: South VietNam
Province: Quang Nam
The Wall: Panel 33W - Row 083

Not a lot of new data, but as I would learn over time, every little bit would come in useful.

Because Mel Canon had initially answered me so quickly, I assumed the rest of the answers would come pouring in equally fast. But I was overly optimistic and over the next few months only made two new contacts. Although they had nothing to do directly with my father, their introduction into my life was as valuable as any other piece of information.

The first person to contact me was Jim Schueckler, a helicopter pilot in Vietnam with the Army's 192nd Assault Helicopter Company, 10th Combat Aviation Battalion. The 192nd's primary job was Combat Assaults, a formation of Hueys (a type of helicopter) that took infantrymen into battle.

To: **Stephanie Hanson**
From: **Jim Schueckler**
Date: *Fri, Nov 15, 1996 2:15pm*

Stephanie,

Mel Canon forwarded your note to me that you were looking for buddies of your Dad.

I have been successful in finding buddies for several relatives of helicopter pilots who were killed in Vietnam. The database of the Vietnam Helicopter Pilots

Association helped me a lot. Finding friends of your Dad's might be a little more difficult, but we can give it a good hard try.

There were 2 Marine Corps helicopters shot down in Quang Nam province on 2/7/69, so there were 4 pilots killed also. I've provided listings of your Dad and the 4 pilots.

I have a database at home that can help me find other KIAs on the same date. I'll also try to find out exactly which of the two helicopters your Dad was on.

As you probably know, Corpsmen were Navy medics who worked with Marine Corps units. They wore Marine uniforms and slept, ate and crawled through the mud with the Marines.

Our most probable contacts will come through posting a note in the newsletter or magazine of the Corpsmen alumni organization. I am not sure there is such an organization, but I'd bet on it. We can also post a note to the newsletter of the Vietnam Helicopter Crew Members Association. (Allied with, but not the same as VHFCN, where Mel already posted a note about you.)

I can post a note for you to the magazine of the Vietnam Veterans of America, but they are many months backlogged.

Any additional information you have, such as what unit he was in or what Marine Corps unit he worked with, could be very helpful.

*I plan to keep in touch with you as we make this
journey together. What I'd like to convey to you is the
bond of brotherhood that existed and still exists between
helicopter crewmen and Vietnam Veterans in general.
Your Dad was like a brother to many of us.*

*On Veterans Day weekend in DC, I met, face-to-face,
several people I have known on the internet for a while,
Mel Canon and many other helicopter pilots, and our
new "Little Sister" Julie Kink.*

*Julie's brother David died in Vietnam. Over the past
few months, Julie found herself becoming the "adopted"
sister of many helicopter pilots. I think she also found
we enjoyed thinking of her that way, too. I CC'd Julie
on this note so the two of you could communicate if you
wish.*

Much Love,
Uncle Jim / Uncle Polecat

My eyes filled with tears as I read Jim's email. This
was a perfect example of the bond of brotherhood that
comes from serving together in war. I don't think it was
possible for Jim to have been kinder or more accepting
of me even if he had served side-by-side with my father.

His attachment contained the names of the four pilots
who had died that day. Two of them had flown with my
father, but we had no way of knowing which two. But I
kept the bit of information to store away.

CPT Bartolina, Ernest E Jr USMC
Last name: BARTOLINA
First name: ERNEST E JR

Date of Casualty: Friday, February 7, 1969
Age at time of loss: 26
Casualty type: (A1) Hostile, died
Reason: Air loss - Crashed on land
      (Pilot - Helicopter)
Country: South VietNam
Province: Quang Nam
The Wall: Panel 33W - Row 075

1LT Glover, Raymond Edward USMC
Last name: GLOVER
First name: RAYMOND EDWARD
Date of Casualty: Friday, February 7, 1969
Age at time of loss: 27
Casualty type: (A1) Hostile, died
Reason: Air loss - Crashed on land
      (Crew member - Helicopter)
Country: South VietNam
Province: Quang Nam
The Wall: Panel 33W - Row 078

1LT Moke, Russell Eugene USMC
Last name: MOKE
First name: RUSSELL EUGENE
Date of Casualty: Friday, February 7, 1969
Age at time of loss: 25
Casualty type: (A1) Hostile, died
Reason: Air loss - Crashed on land
      (Crew member - Helicopter)
Country: South VietNam
Province: Quang Nam
The Wall: Panel 33W - Row 080

1LT Prombo, John Anthony USMC
Last name: PROMBO
First name: JOHN ANTHONY
Date of Casualty: Friday, February 7, 1969
Age at time of loss: 25
Casualty type: (A1) Hostile, died
Reason: Air loss - Crashed on land
      (Pilot - Helicopter)
Country: South VietNam
Province: Quang Nam
The Wall: Panel 33W - Row 081

That same day I received an email from Julie Kink. She shared with me the story of her own search for people that knew her brother, Warrant Officer David Robert Kink, a helicopter pilot with Charlie Troop, 1st Squadron, 9th Cavalry, killed in action on August 3, 1969. Julie was only eight years old when he died and therefore she had few memories of him. Julie was an avid supporter and champion of Vietnam veterans and hearing about her search gave me more courage than she will ever know. It validated approval for my search and other people who felt like I did, plus the right to mourn someone you hadn't known very well or even at all.

Julie understood my every emotion, sometimes before I put my feelings into words. Even when I tried to explain this to her, she was one step ahead of me.

You bet I am right there with you on all the emotions, though our situations are different. We share the common bond of loss so we do understand each other. I feel strongly that your birth dad is proud of you for seeking him out. The guys who were there and didn't come back have to be there in spirit whenever you or I are made happy by finding someone in our search, or whenever there is a reunion of guys slapping each other on the back, remembering being THERE, and the good times as well as the bad. They just have to be witnessing that, somewhere. Or, even directing it, in a way ...

THREE

THERE ARE MANY HEROES IN THIS WORLD YOU never hear about. They don't make the news or national headlines, but they are out there, just living life like Jim Schueckler. He earned the title of hero, as well as the nickname of Uncle Polecat, in his never-ending quest to help me.

For one of his first projects, he created a web page in honor of Gary and posted it on *The Virtual Wall* which he founded in 1997. *The Virtual Wall* provides a place for personal memorials to the men and women who are named on The Wall in Washington, D.C. Visitors may leave tributes, letters, poems and photos for other visitors to view. Their goal is to provide an environment like The Wall itself, with the dignity and respect those named on The Wall have earned, no flashy or noisy distractions, no commercials, no fees to publish a memorial and no hand held out for donations. Gary's memorial page continues to get visitors who contact me to this day.

Jim posted the link to Gary's memorial page every imaginable place. He sent letters to various associations and posted messages on any message board and listing he could find. Although he had limited contacts within the Marine and Navy worlds, he persisted and one day finally came across new information.

> *...Gary was a crew member flying in a USMC CH-46A Sea Knight helicopter. The helo and crew were on a medevac mission and were hit by ground fire. There were 5 on board at the time, all from Gary's unit (HMM-265). They all perished.*
>
> *Also on the same date a CH-46D was downed belonging to a sister unit, HMM-364. It too was lost in Quang Nam Province. There were 4 Americans who died in that crash. I am not sure if the incidents were related.*

But with all of Jim's efforts, months went by with no one contacting me, and I started to lose hope of ever really finding out what happened to my father.

Then on February 6th, a hand-addressed, oversized envelope from a G. Johnson in Takoma Park, Maryland arrived in the mail. I carefully opened the envelope and found a letter inside, along with two additional pieces of paper.

February 1997

Dear Ms. Hanson,

I read Jim Schueckler's post on the VWAR listserve and found the enclosed condolence letter and casualty report at the Nixon Project at the Archives II in College Park, MD. I'm sorry the copy of the casualty report isn't clearer.

*If you have any questions or if I can be of any help,
please contact me.*

*Good Luck,
Gary Johnson*

Gary Johnson, to me, was the perfect definition of a Good Samaritan. To spend time looking through thirty-year-old records because of a few sentences he saw posted on a message board about someone he didn't even know, was truly extraordinary.

The condolence letter was a typed form letter with a stamped-in date and signature.

Feb 20 1969

Dear Mr. Young:

It was with deep regret I learned of the death of your son, Hospitalman Gary N. Young.

I realize the overwhelming grief you are suffering and know how desperately you are seeking to understand the tragic loss of your son. It is sincerely hoped you will find the courage and strength to continue as he would have wanted. Our efforts to bring this conflict to an end will continue so others might be spared your sorrow.

Mrs. Nixon joins me in extending to you our deepest sympathy in the loss of your son and you may be sure you will be remembered in our prayers.

*Sincerely,
Richard Nixon*

The other piece of paper was the Report of Casualty on my father. Written in military jargon, I had difficulty in discerning any new pertinent information.

But one section was titled Interested Persons. It listed my father's relatives as Delbert Lee Newton - stepfather, Weldon Edmond Young - father, and Deceased - mother. The list included Portland addresses for each of the men. Almost three decades old, the information didn't make me change my mind and try to find them.

Then Jim Schueckler called me for the first time and immediately got to the point of his call.

"I received a package from Gary Johnson this evening," he said. "Did you get your copy yet?"

"Actually, I'm reading it right now. I can't believe he went down to the Archives for me."

"This could turn out to be the clue we needed to help you find your family. I spent the last few hours running a search for anyone in the United States whose name matched or came close to Gary's father and stepfather's names listed on this report. I sent it off to you in email. It includes addresses and phone numbers and I realize it may be a long shot, but I think you should begin making calls tomorrow. You do remember what tomorrow is?"

"Yes, the twenty-eighth anniversary of Gary's death. But I don't know if I'm ready to make those calls. What if I just end up hurting them?"

"The family will most likely be thinking of Gary and that might help ease the shock of finding out they have a granddaughter they never knew about. I really think you should do it."

Jim had spent so many hours trying to help me and was so excited about this, I couldn't disappoint him. I promised to make the calls and let him know how it went the next day.

IN THE MORNING, I FOUND JIM'S EMAIL AND printed out the list with hundreds, if not thousands, of names.

Knowing I needed moral support for this, I searched out Shelly Winter and pulled her into an empty office. I showed her the papers Gary Johnson sent me and filled her in on the details of my conversation with Jim.

"When are you going to do this?" she asked.

"Right now, before I lose my nerve. Will you stay with me?"

"I wouldn't miss this for the world." Shelly pulled up a chair and sat down.

I sat down too, and laid out the list of names.

"Who are you calling first? Gary's dad?" Shelly asked.

"No, his stepfather. I remember Linda said he really raised Gary, instead of his dad."

I picked up the phone and randomly picked one of the Delbert Newtons listed in Portland. But the odds of him being the right one were probably about as good as winning the lottery. I started to dial the number, but Shelly stopped me.

"What exactly are you going to say?" she asked.

I pointed to the list. "Shelly, look at all these names. By the time I finally find the right person, I will have figured something out."

Taking a closer look, she agreed and wished me luck. I dialed the number again. An older gentleman answered and I asked to speak with Delbert Newton.

"This is he," he replied.

"I'm looking for a Delbert Newton who was the stepfather of Gary Young who was killed in Vietnam," I said blandly as if reading a script.

"Well, that's me," he answered in a surprised tone.

Oh, God, what was I going to say now? I covered the mouthpiece and frantically whispered, "It's him!"

Thinking Shelly would know what to say, I tried to hand the phone to her, but she shook her head and refused to take it. Several seconds passed while we shoved the phone back and forth, almost like a game of hot potato, until I realized I had left Delbert on the phone in silence. I finally put the phone back up to my mouth. "Umm, my name is Stephanie and I'm Gary's daughter."

I regretted it the moment I blurted it out. I definitely could have found a more tactful approach. How was he supposed to react to a statement like that?

"Well, that's something, isn't it?" he said calmly.

"I'm so sorry. I didn't mean to just say it like that," I apologized.

I gave him an abbreviated version of my adoption and finding my birth mother the year before.

"Do you remember Linda?" I asked.

After a few seconds, he said, "No, I don't recall anyone by that name."

"She is my birth mother and the one who told me Gary is my father. She showed me a picture of Gary and I do look just like him."

"I think you should talk with my younger son, Steve. He might be able to figure this all out. He always knew the same people Gary did. Let me have your phone number and I'll have him call you."

I gave him both my work and home phone numbers. Still embarrassed over the way I had handled this call, I thanked him for being so kind. I don't think many people in this world could have handled my news as graciously.

When the phone call ended, I wondered if finding

Gary's family on the very first phone call was just a twist of fate? Julie's words of someone directing our searches came to mind. Was this yet another nudge pushing me down a path I didn't know about?

Every time the phone rang the rest of the day, I jumped, but as the hours dragged by, I worried perhaps Steve didn't want to talk with me.

But when I arrived home that evening a message on my answering machine from Steve asked that I "please, please call him."

I dialed his number as fast as I could.

When I identified myself, he asked, "What is your mother's name?"

"Linda."

"Well then, this is your Uncle Steve." His voice sounded deep and almost gruff, but also warm and loving. "What took you so long to call me?" he asked jokingly. "But seriously, I've waited for this day for over twenty years."

Startled, I asked, "What do you mean? I didn't think any of you knew I existed. Linda said she never got the chance to tell Gary."

"I saw Linda at Gary's funeral, obviously pregnant. I figured it had to be Gary's child and the next day I confronted her, asking what she was going to do with the baby. She told me she might give it up for adoption, and I begged her to give it to me. But she refused, saying she didn't want her child raised in the shadow of Gary's death.

"I eventually realized it made more sense, as I was only 18 at the time, in the Army and not in a position to raise a child. I haven't seen Linda since that day, but often wondered what happened to Gary's child. And for some reason, I never told anyone else in the family anything about this."

We talked for hours that evening.

"There were three of us in the Young family – Ron, Gary and myself, in that order. Ron already served a tour in Vietnam before Gary went over. His experience changed him immensely and he returned a totally different person. One of his jobs in Vietnam had been to count and keep track of the dead bodies, which affected him deeply. When Gary died, he never recovered from that additional blow.

"One night in 1981, Ron fell asleep on Gary's grave, woke up disoriented and wandered onto the freeway where he was struck and killed by a car."

Steve seemed to have lived a fairly average life albeit devastated by all the losses. Recently married, he had two stepdaughters, but no children of his own. Since Ron also never had children, it meant the Young line all boiled down to me. The only one of my generation.

STEVE AND I MET FOR THE FIRST TIME THE DAY after we initially talked. We met at a pub near his house, where he played pool with his wife and friends.

When I arrived, I headed in the direction of the pool tables. As I got closer, a man stood up and stared at me as if seeing a ghost. I had no doubt it was Steve. Not only because of the way he looked at me, but because I saw a grown-up version of my father. Without speaking a word, we hugged, and a calmness swept over me. I was with my family and it felt like coming home.

After he introduced me to Kim, his wife, he and I sat down at a table to have a private talk.

"I can't believe how much you look like Gary," Steve said. "Especially your eyes and your smile. Most definitely your smile."

"Yeah, I always hated that crooked look, but the minute I saw Gary's picture, I knew I would never hate it again," I replied.

"And you have Linda's hair and eye color."

"What was Gary's coloring?" I asked. "The only picture I have is from the newspaper."

"His eyes were the most brilliant green. People always seemed to remember his eyes. And he had sandy-colored hair that turned really blond in the summer when he got tan."

Although we danced around the topic of Gary's death, inevitably it came up.

"Gary was over in Vietnam for almost five months. He worked in a hospital of sorts for most of the time. But then he transferred to a different unit to fly medevac missions." Steve paused for a moment to compose himself. "He was killed on his first mission."

Killed on his very first mission? How devastating and ironic, like many of the stories from Vietnam. A boy killed while filling in for someone else's mission. Or killed the first day he got there, or the day before he was to leave. I knew there were thousands of similar stories, but this time my father was one of those statistics.

I asked Steve about the crash, preparing myself to finally hear what really happened to my father. But to my astonishment, Steve only knew what the newspapers had written.

"We never did find out any more details. All we ever really knew was the helicopter crashed and all of the men were killed."

Disappointment overwhelmed me. For some reason I needed to hear the details from that day, and I thought Steve would have the answers. It's difficult to explain, not knowing what questions I even wanted answered, but knowing there was more information out there somewhere. But if the family was never told the details, would it ever be possible for me to find it? Would I ever learn what happened to my father?

AFTER HOURS OF TALKING, STEVE ASKED ME TO come over to his house to look at the pictures he kept of Gary. Their living room had one wall full of pictures – and the majority of them were of Gary. Steve spent quite a while explaining each picture, and the adoration he had for his older brother was heart-warming. And seeing other pictures of my father just confirmed how much I looked like him.

At one point, Steve apologized for not having anything else of Gary's to show me.

"But we do have a box of Gary's things up in Delbert's attic," he said. "When we go over there tomorrow, we'll get it down and you can look at anything you like. I wouldn't be surprised if Delbert just gives it to you."

"I couldn't possibly take it away from you guys," I protested.

"I don't see why not. None of it has been touched for years. He has one of Gary's medals and the flag that covered his coffin in a special place, but I'll bet he gives the rest of it to you."

I really didn't want to take anything away from the family, except possibly one thing – Gary's dog tags. I'd had a fascination with dog tags for several years. It started years before when my brother, Geoff, gave me a Danielle Steel book set during the Vietnam War and strangely enough, the only book he ever gave me. In that book, the main character wore the dog tags of her fiancé who had been killed in Vietnam. I guess this idea always stuck with me, because when Geoff went over to the Gulf, I asked for his dog tags. He gave them to me, although I'm sure he got into a lot of trouble for doing so, and I wore them until the day he came back home.

"You know, there is one thing I would really love to have if you guys didn't mind," I confessed. "Do you still have Gary's dog tags?"

Steve thought for a minute and said, "I don't think I ever saw them. I don't think they sent them back. Or if they did, we didn't keep them."

I tried not to show him how much his answer hurt, but he noticed how it upset me.

"Wait a minute, I do have something of Gary's!" he exclaimed.

He went into his bedroom and came out with something in his closed fist.

"Hold out your hand," he said.

I did and he placed the face of a watch in it.

"That was Gary's watch he wore over in Vietnam. He probably was wearing it the day he died, because it returned broken."

It struck me I was touching something my father had touched. We sat in silence looking down at my hand. All of a sudden Steve jumped as if startled, his face pale and his eyes never leaving my hand.

"The watch is working," he said in a strained voice.

I frowned because I didn't understand why that would spook him so much.

"I always planned to get it fixed so I could wear it. But when I finally got around to it, they couldn't get it to work. Now the second I put it in your hand it starts ticking again."

Twenty-eight years after my father's death, the thought made me shiver.

FOUR

I'M HAPPY TO ADMIT I WAS WRONG IN THINKING it would be easier on Gary's family if I didn't find them. Although I know it is difficult at times to have a constant reminder of my father around, Steve and Delbert have never once shown anything but joy from the moment I came into their lives.

My biological grandparents, Weldon and Jewell Young, divorced when Steve was about two years old. Jewell married Delbert Newton, who became the boys' stepfather. However, Weldon seldom came into the picture, and Delbert became the true father figure in their lives. Although Delbert and Jewell divorced many years later, and Jewell passed away when Gary was in boot camp, Delbert maintained the status of "Pops" in Steve's life.

When I first met Delbert in February of 1997, he took one look at me, turned to Steve and whispered in his ear, then they both burst into laughter. Steve's wife, Kim, pressed them to repeat what they laughed about.

Steve finally answered, "When I talked to Delbert after Stephanie called, he was still a bit skeptical Gary had a kid he didn't know about. He said if I had any doubts about her claim, I could take her for a blood test.

When he saw Stephanie today all he had to say was 'Well, I guess there's no need for that blood test!'"

The love Delbert still had for Gary was evident when he left the room, and came back carrying two items with great care. He sat down next to me and opened a small, old and faded blue box. Inside lay Gary's Purple Heart medal. Taking it out of the box, he placed it in my hand. I had never held a military medal before and the weight surprised me. The regal and dignified Purple Heart medal is awarded for injury or death in combat. It's literally purple in the shape of a heart with a gold border and the engraving of George Washington's profile on the front. On the back, below the words "For Military Merit," Gary's name was engraved.

He showed me the other item, the folded American flag, which draped Gary's coffin. While I mulled over these items, Delbert went back upstairs and eventually came down with another box, containing what was left of Gary's possessions.

Delbert had a wide array of items, from Gary's sailor hat, to a shaving kit containing an old razor and empty bottle of Old Spice aftershave, to his address book. None of the items could be called valuable, but to me they were priceless.

I pulled out a brown leather wallet and opened it, expecting to see the usual items. This one was only full of pictures, almost exclusively of girls.

Steve laughed. "Gary was the only guy I ever knew who could crook his finger at a girl and she would come over. He had an undeniable charm."

A square jewelry box held the 1966 class pin from Wilson High School. After finding out the family didn't have Gary's dog tags, I hoped maybe he had a class ring. When I saw the class pin, I struggled not to let my disappointment show. It may sound silly, but I longed for something of my father's I could wear every day.

One of the most interesting items was Gary's boot camp yearbook called "The Anchor." I opened it and tried to find Gary in the multitude of pictures, but soon realized the majority of them were stock photos. Near the back I found the individual shots for his company - Company 67-275. Near the bottom of the page I saw his picture; a solemn picture almost as fascinating as his senior year picture. In this shot without the smile, I could see I had his full lips and realized we didn't have just matching grins, but identical mouths.

Steve searched farther in the box. Suddenly, in a strangled voice he said, "Um, Stephanie."

In his hand hung a single dog tag. I knew instantly Gary had worn this when he died. My eyes filled with tears and without saying a word, I took it from Steve's hand and clenched it in my fist never wanting to let go.

Steve glanced at Delbert. "I don't think you should try to take it away from her. It might be dangerous."

"I'm happy to let you keep the tags, Stephanie," Delbert said warmly. "Actually you can just take home the whole box."

"Oh, I can't do that to you guys," I protested.

"But it belongs with you now. Actually it all belongs to you now, but I think I'll just borrow the medal and the flag for a while longer."

"You can keep them for as long as you want and if you ever want anything back from this box, just ask and you'll get it."

The mood in the room had become tearfully sentimental, so I closed the box and turned the conversation to more pleasant things, knowing I could now study all the items later.

AT HOME, I IMMEDIATELY PULLED EVERYTHING out of the box and sorted it into groups. A slim envelope contained a few family pictures of Gary as a baby and again showed the remarkable similarities to my own baby pictures. The whole facial structure was identical from the chubby cheeks, the nose, the chin, even down to the teeth. Although I was beginning to get used to the idea of looking so much like someone else, it was still spooky to see this.

I found eleven black and white pictures Gary took in Vietnam. Most of them buildings, I assumed they were the places where he worked and lived. I would have to try to get someone to tell me exactly what they were. To my chagrin, there weren't any pictures of Gary himself over there.

A Western Union telegram stated the official notice of Gary's death.

I deeply regret to confirm on behalf of the United States Navy that your son HN Gary Norman Young, USN, B82 47 67 was killed in action on 7 February 1969 seven miles NW of An Hoa, Quang Nam, South Vietnam when the helicopter on which he was a crew member was on an emergency medevac mission and came under intense small arms and automatic weapons fire and crashed in the landing zone.

Your son died while serving his country. I extend to you my sincere sympathy in your great loss.

A letter from his Commanding Officer setting forth the circumstances of death will follow. I wish to assure you of every possible assistance.

If you desire and at no expense to you we will prepare and casket the remains and transport them with an escort to any place you designate.

Also we will allow you an amount toward funeral and interment expenses not to exceed five hundred dollars if interment is in a private cemetery, or two hundred fifty dollars if remains are assigned to a funeral director prior to interment in a national cemetery, or seventy-five dollars if remains are consigned directly to a national cemetery.

Please wire collect Bureau of Medicine and Surgery, Department of the Navy, Washington DC 20390 the name of the national cemetery or funeral establishment to which remains are to be sent.

Should you desire any information concerning the casket or preparation and transportation of remains please contact the Bureau of Medicine and Surgery, Department of the Navy.

Vice Admiral C K Duncan
Chief of Naval Personnel

And of course, there were the official condolence letters. I read the ones from Gary's officers in Vietnam first.

MARINE AIR BASE SQUADRON 16
Marine Aircraft Group 16
1st Marines Aircraft Wing, FMFPac
FPO San Francisco, 96602

February 9, 1969

Dear Mr. Newton,

It is difficult for me to express the sense of loss and sorrow felt by his many friends in this Squadron over the recent death of your step-son, Hospitalman Gary N. Young B824767, U. S. Navy on February 7th, 1969, in the vicinity of DaNang, Republic of Vietnam.

Gary was flying as Corpsman on the CH-46 Medical Evacuation helicopter in support of numerous ground units stationed in the province. An emergency call was received, requesting the MEDEVAC helicopter to pick up a critically wounded Marine in the delta area southwest of DaNang. While attempting to land the helicopter was subjected to intense hostile gunfire causing it to crash. The crash was witnessed by Marine troops on the ground and by the escort helicopter. Ground troops were dispatched to the crash site immediately. If it is any consolation, there is no doubt the occupants died instantaneously, and I can assure you Gary was spared any suffering.

Gary was an outstanding Hospital Corpsman and was liked and respected by the Doctors and fellow Corpsmen with whom he worked. His voluntary flights on MEDEVAC missions attested to his courage and his willingness to perform above and beyond the requirement of duty. His cheerful outlook, devotion to duty and courageous acceptance of the hazards of his work won him the respect of all.

It may comfort you to know a memorial service will be

held at the Marble Mountain Air Facility Chapel for
Gary on February 11, 1969. If I may be of assistance to
you in any possible way, please do not hesitate to write.

> *Sincerely,*
> *Wm. Cunningham*
> *Lieutenant Colonel,*
> *U. S. Marine Corps*

Delbert confirmed Steve's memory of Gary being killed on his first mission, but this letter referred to missions, as in plural. Was it possible Gary flew more than once? Unfortunately, the other letters did not shed more light onto this question. But one of them did answer a question Jim Schueckler and I had from the beginning.

GROUP CHAPLAIN'S OFFICE
Marine Aircraft Group Sixteen
1st Marine Aircraft Wing
Aircraft, FMF, Pacific
C/O Fleet Post Office
San Francisco, California 96602

12 February 1969

Dear Mr. Newton,

Please accept my deepest sympathy to you on the recent
loss of your stepson, Hospitalman Gary Norman
Young, USN. I know that you have already received
official word from the Navy Department, but I wish to
send my personal condolences and the knowledge of my
prayers.

We conducted a memorial service for your stepson and the men who were flying with him. This service was on 11 February at the Marine Aircraft Group Sixteen Chapel. Almost two hundred men of his squadron attended the service to honor him. I felt you would want a copy of the memorial service bulletin.

As a chaplain here in Vietnam, I assure you your stepson did not give his life in vain. He was highly motivated in his efforts to help the wounded and made special efforts to volunteer for this Medical Evacuation work. He gave his full measure of devotion in the defense of the country he loved and for the protection of his family at home. Our prayers were for you and for all the men whose lives are in constant danger in the service of their country.

May God richly bless you and inspire you to seek His Spirit for help in the days ahead.

> *Yours in the Spirit of Christ,*
> *G. Bruce Schumacher*
> *Chaplain, U. S. Navy*
> *Marine Aircraft Group-16*

I pulled the memorial service bulletin the chaplain referred from the box, and saw the typed program listing the names the service was held for.

ERNEST ELBERT BARTOLINA, JR.
Captain USMC

RUSSELL EUGENE MOKE
First Lieutenant USMC

CHARLES WILLARD MILLER, JR.
Corporal USMC

RODNEY GEORGE SHANK
Lance Corporal USMC

WALTER RIPLEY TYRRELL
Hospitalman USN

GARY NORMAN YOUNG
Hospitalman USN

So the pilots of Gary's helicopter were Bartolina and Moke. On the back side of the program, another listing of the men gave their hometown address and those who survived them. Only the two pilots had been married, and none of them listed any children as survivors.

There were other condolence letters, including ones from the Secretary of the Navy, the Mayor of Portland, the Chief of Naval Operations, etc. But they were all form letters with no specific information about Gary or the crash.

The huge stack of personal condolence letters, cards and telegrams attested to the popularity of Gary and how much he was loved. One of these letters, from Mrs. Dorothy Moke, the mother of Russell Moke, caught my eye. In addition to her condolences, she included a newspaper clipping written on her son.

E. Peorian Killed In Vietnam

A 25-year-old East Peoria Marine was killed Friday in Vietnam when the helicopter he co-piloted was shot down while on an evacuation mission.

First Lt. Russell E. (Butch) Moke, son of Mr. and Mrs. S. Russell Moke, had been in Vietnam only three weeks. He sustained injuries to his head and body when the helicopter was hit by small arms and automatic weapon fire while approaching the landing zone to evacuate wounded soldiers. He was killed near An Hoa, Quang Nam Province.

Born in Peoria Jan. 19, 1944, Lt. Moke attended East Peoria Community High School and graduated from St. Bede's College in Peru. He also attended Bradley University before joining the U.S. Marine Corps three years ago.

Surviving besides his parents are his wife, Dianne, and infant daughter, both of Pensacola, Fla.; a sister and other relatives in the East Peoria area.

Lt. Moke, his wife and daughter, had visited relatives over the Christmas holidays before he left for Vietnam.

Oh, he also had a daughter like me! I would love to talk to her, but the letter didn't even mention her name. Did she wonder what happened to her father like I did?

The last items were letters from Gary. I had put them aside, knowing they would be the most difficult for me, and finally I got up the courage to read them. Only eight in all, I read them in chronological order.

Gary wrote the first few while he was at Camp Pendleton and working at the Naval Hospital. The main subjects were his car, his lack of money and how much he missed Portland. Typical guy letters.

The rest were sent from Vietnam, the first one dated three months after his arrival. Steve said Gary sent home more letters than this, but they must have gotten misplaced or thrown away over the years. But I was grateful for any personal insight to my father the remaining letters gave me.

All but the last letter had the same return address of MAG-11, First Marine Air Squadron, Medical Section, the dispensary in DaNang, where he worked before volunteering for medevac missions. All the letters were addressed to Delbert, with the exception of one sent to Gary's brother, Ron, less than three weeks before he died. It was the only letter in which Gary expressed his true feelings and fears and perhaps that was because Ron already served a tour in Vietnam.

January 24, 1969

Dear Ron,

How is it going brother? What's this about me owing you a letter or three? They sure mustn't have gotten here, 'cause I sure didn't get them. Dad said he sent a couple of tapes, but they never got here. I don't know what it is.

How is life back in the world? I have just about lost all my senses over here. We got the hell knocked out of us last Wed. I'm not kidding, I never ran so fast nor so hard for the bunker when the shit started coming in. We lost one of the Corpsmen here. He got shrapnel in the neck. It was curtains for him. There wasn't much we could do for him. He needed whole blood, and we didn't have it.

Hanoi Hannah said over the radio we were going to

catch hell again tonight. Ha, she asked if DaNang was ready to give up yet. Okay bitch. She has been pretty good in her predictions so far. Sometimes I wonder if she isn't out there humping those rockets up to be fired. Grand old lady!!

Well, so far no hearts. I will be happy if I leave this place just like I came ... in one piece. Preferably alive. Cheez, I can't wait to get out of this place. It will be so great to set my feet down on American soil. It will be even better when I hit the Portland airport. Damn, I will be so excited I won't know what to do. I just sit and wonder what it will be like to go home. I think I'm slowly, but surely, going out of my mind. It wouldn't surprise me all that much.

What have you been up to? Dad said you were thinking of going to school full time. That will be kind of tough won't it? I sure can't wait to get out of the service and start school. There are so many things I want to do and need to accomplish. I just welcome the opportunity and challenge. It will be kind of nice to address me as a civilian again. Wow!

Hope you all had a great Christmas. I hope to be with you all next year. I didn't have the best Christmas I have ever had, but it was to be expected. I made the best of it as I could.

I'm sitting here on a Friday night. I was lucky enough to get hold of this typewriter. What a way to spend a Friday night. Oh well, I will make up for this entire tour as soon as I get back to the states and start to live like a human again.

As Dad has probably told you, I am trying to purchase a new sports car. I sure hope the deal works out okay, as it sure would be great to have the thing waiting for me when I get back. Wow. Can you feature me in a new sports car with the shades and all? I could dig it. We will have to make it down to the beach about twelve dozen times. Boy, just thinking about it makes me smile. It seems so far away, but the time will pass quickly, I know.

In less than a month, I am pretty sure I will be moving up to MAG-39, which is in Quang Tri. It is 15 miles away from the DMZ. I will be flying on Med-Evacs. I can't wait. It should be interesting and it is just that much more pay (flight pay). It will also make the time pass quicker, as flying is really time consuming.

Well, I had better go for now, Ron. Hope you can find the time to write back. I know I'm the world's worst typist, but I will try to do better next time. I just wanted you to know I was thinking of ya, and as always, I miss you and everyone so very, very much. Take care of yourself and you had better start preparing Portland for my return. That town just won't be the same. Gotta go and get ready for tonight. Take care and I will do the same. Waiting for the day I get back.

See you later,
Love, Gar

When I read this letter, I got the feeling as if Gary had a premonition something was going to happen, and by writing down his future plans, he could prevent it. Years later, one of Gary's best friends from high school told me

Gary knew he wasn't coming home. At his send-off at the Portland Airport, Gary pulled him aside and told him he knew he was seeing everyone for the last time. Linda confirmed Gary also confided these same fears to her. Learning this made his last letters that much more poignant.

The very last letter had "New Address" written on the envelope and came from MAG-16. It was the same return address as on the condolence letters from the Commanding Officer and Chaplain from MAG-16.

4 February '69

Dear Dad,

Just a real short note to let you know I have a new address. I am now with MAG-16. It's helicopter squadron.

I will be flying on Med-Evac choppers. I will write later & fill you in on all the details.

Please write if ya get a chance. I won't be able to send any more tapes for awhile. This place is so desolate. Gotta go for now & get squared away. Hope to be flying soon.

Love,
Gar

And three days later he died. Without getting the chance to really live out his dream of flying medevacs. I put all the items back into the box and wiped away my tears. Although he died twenty-eight years before, for me it was as if he just died. I put his dog tags on and sat for hours wishing I had known him and he had known me.

AFTER OUR INITIAL MEETING, I REGULARLY visited both Steve and Delbert. Every once in a while, Delbert would find a new picture or token of Gary's to give to me. In this manner, I received his high school yearbook, copies of his graduation invitation and all sorts of other neat memorabilia. He also mentioned he had tapes somewhere, but after several months, I lost hope of ever seeing them. Then one morning Delbert called me at work.

"Stephanie, I finally dug up the taped letters Gary sent home from Vietnam," he said. "I transferred some of the reel-to-reel tapes to cassette tape and you can come get them anytime."

An adrenaline rush went through me to think I would actually hear my father's voice.

When I picked up the tapes, Delbert said emotionally, "I tried not to listen to them as I transferred them. I would hit the start button and then run out of the room. But at times I did hear his voice."

I couldn't have felt more grateful for Delbert's difficult effort for me and realized this would be the closest I would ever get to my father.

"I have no idea why I saved them all these years," Delbert said. "I knew I would never listen to them again."

"I guess you were keeping them for me, even if you didn't know it at the time."

As I drove back to work, I told myself to wait until I got home to listen to the tapes. But when I arrived at my office building, I sat in the parking lot staring at the tapes and knew I couldn't wait five more hours.

The tapes didn't have any dates on them, so I chose one at random and slid it into my tape deck. I could hear the whirling of the tape and after a few seconds, I heard my father's voice, kind and full of life and laughter. And I felt like I had known the voice all my life.

Hi Pops,

Got the tapes today and boy, it sure sounds good to hear those voices again. Still, I say it's better than getting a letter - almost like getting a telephone call.

Kind of happy today because last night I went to Thailand. Thailand is a pretty nice place. Went over there for just overnight, but believe me, I didn't get much sleep. Good to get away from this place for a change. This place can really get a guy down. Had some real good food for a change. First food I've had in 'bout a month and a half that's halfway tasty. Rode around in these rickshaws all over town. Think I paid about 13 cents. There's a money conversion over there. You have to change our money into what they call bot. 5 bot is worth a quarter. So at times I was kind of confused as to how much to give a guy. Worked out in the end I guess.

This morning I was just making a list of the things I really miss and thought I would kind of relay them to you. All right, these may not be in order of preference, but they are all on the list.

- One is a good shower.
- A toilet that flushes.
- Some good food. I think that's probably pretty close to

the top. Some real good food. Instead of Marine food.
Boy, that can really get you down after a while.
- Going to chow and sitting down without a .45
strapped to your side.
- And another thing I'd like to see, or hear, is a
telephone that rings. All the telephones over here are all
field telephones. All they do is just buzz. Gets kind of
nerve-racking after a while.
- Another thing I would like to see is a pair of shoes.
These boots are getting kind of old, much less trying to
get a little heavy.
- Think another thing I miss over here is good-tasting
water. All the water over here is contaminated and they
have to put so much chlorine in it, it just loses all the
original taste. Like the water over out at Ma's. Boy, I
never tasted such good water. Good, fresh well-water.
- Another thing is American greenbacks. Over here in
Vietnam we have what we call military payment
certificates and due to inflation, we can't bring
American money into the country, so we have to use
what they call funny money. Gets kind of old carrying
all this money around. All your change is in paper and
it's different from what you're used to in the States.
- Oh yeah. How could I forget this? (Laugh) Number
one of course is American girls. Ah heck, I'm not even
particular. Anything with round eyes. Just to take a
look, at least.

I'm stationed with about 20 other corpsmen here. Every
once in a while, I get to go out on what they call
MedCap patrols. We go out to the villages and treat the
people. And they call corpsmen or doctors "bacsi." And
as far as they're concerned, bacsi is Number One. They
come to the villages and they treat them and they (the

Vietnamese people) they just treat the bacsi with so much respect – it's truly unbelievable. And you have such a feeling of self-satisfaction when you treat these people, because you know these are the ones that need it the most.

They have a plan over here for service men who want to extend for six months after the original 13 months. At the end of the 13 months you can get a free round-trip ticket to anywhere in the free world. You could go to Australia, Germany, or if you wanted to, you could go back to the States. I've been thinking of seriously looking into it. If I had to say right now, I'd probably just, after my 13 months, just come home and forget all about it. But it's not all that bad over here. It's kind of nerve-racking once in a while, but the money's good, so I really can't complain. I could use some good chow though. (Laugh) But I have been thinking of looking into it. Probably be the only chance to go someplace in the world besides if I had to pay for it. Was thinking of going either to Europe or to Switzerland. Be a good experience, but 18, 19 months away from home is a long time.

Here's another corpsman stationed with me. His name's Willy. George Williams is his real name, I think. So here, he has a few words to say about this wonderful country:

"You want me to talk now? Gee, I don't know what to say. This place is just so great. I've been here for a whole month or so now. It's not really too bad. (Is this to your girl? To your dad?) Well, we're taking good care of Gary over here. Guess I can say that. Guess he's

*told you he's on the football team. He's pretty good too.
There you go."*

*Thank you, Willy. I guess I failed to mention the
football team I'm on over here. It's the squadron football
team and when it's not raining over here, and we have
the free time and we're not getting hit by rockets -
which is seldom - we go out and play. I'm playing
quarterback right now. Played one game and won it 28-
2. I threw four touchdowns passes which made me feel
pretty happy. Some pretty good guys are over here. I
think, so far since I've been in the service, the best men
are over here in Vietnam. We're all lonely and waiting
to get home, but I think it's a pretty united group and
everyone sticks up for everyone else. 'Cause we all feel
the same way. It's a pretty tight group.*

*As I've mentioned, I work seven days a week and every
third day I work 36 hours straight. And as I said, it
helps the time go by pretty quick. Let's see.
Approximately, I've been here for about 40 days, six
hours and 19, no 20 seconds. That's approximate of
course, you know. (Laugh) I don't know. The time
seems to be going by pretty quick. Still, I've got almost
a year to go and it looks pretty far off. I'll sure be one
happy guy when that 13 months is up come next
October ...*

Barely able to see through my tears, I reached down
and shut the tape off. It was just too much for me to hear
when I knew I had to go back to work.

When I finally got home that evening, I played the
tape from where I had left off earlier in the day.

...Don't really know how to describe this country. It's kind of a mixture. Places are flat and bare and just like deserts almost and other places are just like, the densest jungles you can imagine. I'd say most of the fighting occurs in the jungle and the rice paddies. It's an unconventional war and these Vietnamese people, the Viet Cong, they know what they're doing. Actually this is their kind of war we're fighting and it kind of hinders us, but I think we're doing a pretty good job over here.

The DaNang area hasn't been hit with rockets, I'd say, for about two weeks now. There's a suspected buildup of North Vietnamese Army and Viet Cong around the area. Kind of hope they haven't got anything planned for us. (Laugh) I hear from the other guys who were here last February about the Tet Assault on the DaNang area. And they've always said that DaNang is one of the strong points of South Vietnam they would really like to get hold of. As far as I'm concerned, you know, they can stay up north for as long as they want. (Laugh)

I don't know if I told you about my mustache, but about a week ago, I whacked it all off. I don't know; everybody tries it over here once in a while, and I guess I tried it. And I had enough of it. I'd like to try to grow a full beard. Unfortunately, my CO just can't see that. Well, looks like this is the end of this side of the tape, so I'll flip it over and see what I can conjure up on the other side. Hang on a second, now ...

Ok, this is side two. I really can't think of much to say, but we'll see what comes out. Sure are a lot of good buys on things over here. I think one of the better-valued things is a tape recorder. They've got an Aiki *tape recorder which costs $228 here. If you were to purchase one of these back in the States it would run well over $450. It's a good-sounding tape, but I kind of doubt if I'm going to pick me up one of them. I want to save my money as much as I can so I can try to get a sports car when I get back. Hey Pop, have you sold my car yet? If so, how much did you get for it?*

I don't know if you can hear this rain and thunder in the background, but it's really carrying on right now. Well, I sure am tired. As I said, last night I went over to Thailand and didn't get any sleep at all, hardly. And tonight I have duty, so that means I work all night tonight and all day tomorrow. Oh the toils. Hah! Betcha feel real sorry for me, don't ya?

Yesterday I had my teeth worked on a little bit. I had a small cavity. That's one good thing about the service is you have all your medical and your dental care and just about everything else paid for. A lot of guys use this as and, I guess you could call it an excuse, no, not an excuse but as a reason to stay in the service. I don't know. I just really can't see it. I've just got too much to do and too much to accomplish on the outside. I want to go to school and I want to get a secure future. Ah, I just can't wait to get out and start going to school and get in my studies. I think the best years of my life will be in college. I just can't wait.

I'm sorry I haven't been writing as much as I should, but with all the stuff going on around here it's really been busy. Went to Freedom Hill, Hill 327 over here on the west side of DaNang. Stayed there for four days and we really got a lot accomplished and were busy all the time. Ran out of food so we had to eat the Vietnamese villager's food which was quite an experience.

The other day I got to do a digital block on this Marine's finger. It's on the same purpose as a dentist giving Novocain. What we use is Zydacain. We have to find the nerves in the finger, they run just on the lateral on the finger, and we had to shoot it with Zydacain so we could take this guy's fingernail off. I don't know. If I was back in the States, I would never get a chance to do this. Been doing quite a bit of suturing over here and surprising myself how fast I catch on. There's so much to learn. You just can't go in there and just sew up a guy. It's a lot more complicated than that.

I really welcome the challenge to learn as much as I can over here. The doctors are real good, as I've said before, and anything we don't understand, they'll take time and explain it to us.

Been getting a few pictures over here. Last night I took a couple pictures in Thailand. Started a little scrapbook and I'll see what I can do with it. Got a few pictures of the jets taking off and a few pictures of the people, the Vietnamese people. I was thinking of getting some pictures of the casualties, but I really don't want to be reminded of it when I do get back to the United States. So I just decided to stay away from it and just take pictures of the things I'd like to remember about my tour here in Vietnam.

All of us over here are pretty confused about the Presidential Campaign that's going back on in the States. There's so many promises made and you hear about this war that's going to be stopped just like that if a man gets elected to the Presidency and it's kind of demoralizing over here because I think we can....oh, I don't know. I think we are going to be here for a lot longer than most people expect and right now I can't see an end to this war.

These people over here, the South Vietnamese people, are, I'd say about 50 to 75 years behind times. Just like a primitive world. As I said, I just can't imagine them surviving here without the help of the United States Forces. We're doing so much good over here and although the guys don't really care to be over here, they all have a lot of pride in partaking and helping these people. And, the people, they really appreciate it.

I got a military driver's license the other day and you ought to see our ambulance. It's just one big crackerbox. It's a 1906 special or something, I'm not sure.

Speaking of driver's license, Dad, have you got a form for sending in for a new driver's license for me? Mine expires in probably a couple of weeks or something. I'd appreciate it if you could send it over here so I could sign it and I'll send it back to you and I'll give you money for the new license so it won't be expired when I get home.

The other day, I ran into another corpsman I knew at Camp Pendleton. Kind of funny to run into someone you know. Kind of makes you feel good. We had a nice little chat and swapping stories. I told him the latest news I knew about Camp Pendleton and I guess he has been over here for about three or four months now. Jed Christman, Judi Christman's twin brother, is home now for 30 days leave and he should be back here, oh I'd said first part of November. We're going to spend Christmas together and I think it's going to help out to know someone here.

Well Pops, the end of the tape's here, so I'd better run.

The next tape had been recorded in September of 1968, probably the first tape he sent home.

Hiya Pop,

Well, I've been here about three weeks now and kinda seems like time is flying by, but then I look ahead and still have a full year here. It's not too encouraging. Sure do miss all of you at home. Sure appreciate all the letters and the tapes. Sure helps out over here, believe me.

It's not too bad over here. Every once in a while, well in fact, it's just about a nightly occurrence now, we get rockets and mortars in. Got bunkers all over the place lined up with sandbags, so whenever we get hit we just go running for the bunkers. So far, been pretty lucky, nothing's been real close. Quite a few guys have been injured and killed around here, but the ones that are injured, they usually come to sick bay here.

Been getting a lot of experience in sewing people up, a lot of first aid. The doctors over here are just outstanding, you can't believe it.

I was pretty lucky to get this tape recorder to play as well as record one back to you. It's one of the doctor's here, he let me come in his little private room and listen to it and record back. At the time, I'm at a dispensary and mostly it's all first-aid work – I'm doing a few minor surgeries. Very minor, I must put in. But it's all so fascinating. You never stop learning. I think that's one of the better things about this field of work. It's going to be, I hope, a short year over here. As I say, the time's going fairly quick. We're always busy. We're working seven days a week. I'm on a three-section duty at the present right now. Besides seven days a week, every third night I work 36 hours. Gets kinda tiring, but time goes by pretty quick.

On the flight over here from California, we left from Travis Air Force Base which is right next to San Francisco. Took us about four hours and we got over to Hawaii, stopped there, refueled, stayed there for about an hour in the Hawaii Airport. At least I can say I was in Hawaii at one time or another. Then from there, we flew on in to Okinawa, which I believe took nine hours. It's quite a trip. Got in to Okinawa on the 9th, I think, of September. We left early in the morning on the 11th. We were mustering all hours of the day and night trying to catch a flight to go on in to DaNang. We were on working parties and not really too much fun. When we left Okinawa, we stopped in the Philippines, Clark Air Force Base. Stopped there for about an hour-and-a-half. Refueled and resupplied, picked up more troops. While I was there, I called Pete McKillip - you know, Moe's brother. He's stationed there at the Naval Communications Center. His wife Kathy is over there with now. He's going to be stationed there probably until about next March, I believe. And if I'm lucky, I'll try to take R&R (rest and relaxation) right around February, I think. I'm not sure, but if I can, I'm going to try to get over there and see them. Be kinda good to see a familiar face.

Last Saturday night I had duty, and when we have duty, we sleep here in the sickbay. At about five o'clock in the morning, we caught about six rockets and they were kinda close. In fact, one hit so close to sickbay it actually shook me out of my rack. Must have been quite a sight, scrambling for the bunker with nothing but my skivvies on.

Hey Pop? Now this is important. Get a notepad and write this down. I want some salmon. Nah. God, I miss it so much. Betcha I ate half that tray when I was home during my 30 days leave. Sure was good and I sure would like some. Probably spoil though, on the way over.

I take a malaria pill once a week. As a matter of fact, I'd better go in there and take mine pretty quick; today's the day. And there's quite a few plague cases over here. We got a report there are six cases of plague over on the west side of DaNang. Quite a few rats and rodents over here and quite a few of the Vietnamese people are getting bitten by them.

As much as I dislike this place, I can feel proud to say I'm over here helping people. These people are so very, very tired of war and poverty. They live in scum. It's worse, I think, than the ghettos back home. So filthy. We're trying to do our best, but because of the lack of personnel over here, it's awful hard to get around to all the people.

Whenever we have time, I try to get in the villages and treat the people. Truly interesting. The people over here really appreciate it. It's really hard to tell the difference between a gook and a regular Vietnamese person over here. They both look alike. Sometimes you don't know if you are treating a gook who will turn around and shoot you the next day, or if you are really helping the people that need the help.

Monsoon season is starting to set in. Boy, you ought to see the rain. Just comes down in buckets and it just doesn't stop for days and days. Nothing like the Oregon weather.

You're going to hear these clicks off and on throughout the tape, because I have to keep turning it off trying to think of something to say. Kinda doubt if I'll make it a whole hour's worth.

Not really much to do over here for entertainment. Usually when I get off work, I try to catch up on my letter writing or every once in a while, I'll go down to the club and have a beer or two. Not really too exciting. Soon as I got over here, I volunteered to fly on the Med Evacuation helicopters, but unfortunately this Marine Air Group doesn't fly 'em. Possibly in two months, I'll be able to transfer to MAG-39 or MAG-16 which fly the Medevac choppers. Kinda looking forward to that. Think it would be kinda interesting.

Boy, you can believe I'm going to be one happy guy

when I get back to the States. Although it's a long ways
away, still looking forward to it. It's gonna feel kinda
good circling the Portland Airport. On the way back,
it's just like the reverse routine, have to stop at
Okinawa and get processed. Probably take two days.
Probably fly on straight into California. Probably be
detained there for about 24 hours at the most and then
I'll head on home for 30 days leave. Then I'll be
stationed somewhere in the States.

It's gonna be kinda tough over here during the
holidays. It won't even seem like it. But there's still
plenty more Christmases to come.

Every once in a while, the corpsman here get a chance
to fly to Thailand. It's kinda like a small Hong Kong.
From what I've heard from the guys, it's real nice.
Looking forward to going over there. At least it'll be a
break to get away from this place.

Quite a few of the guys here at the dispensary are
getting pretty short. One guy is leaving tomorrow
morning and a couple of the guys are leaving next week
and we should be getting some new guys in pretty
soon. At least I won't feel like low man on the totem
pole any more.

I should pick up another rank up to E-4 while I'm over
here. Possible, but very improbable I'll pick up E-5.
Soon as I go over two years, which is in May, I'll be
getting another pay raise, another boost in the check. It
will help out quite a bit. And when I get home, as I say,
I'll have quite a bit of money. I just keep thinking about
that little sports car. It will be good to get around in.

I'll probably pay all cash for it, but if not, I'll just make my monthly payments on it. Anyway, I should be able to swing it one way or the other.

Wish I had a nickel for every shot I've given over here. Boy, I'd be a rich man; I could retire soon as I got back in the States. Done a lot of suturing, putting stitches in. The other day I sewed up a Colonel. He had a laceration on the chin from some shrapnel. He was pretty lucky it didn't take his whole head off. I told him I would send him my bill at the first of the month. (Laugh)

Most of the guys over here are pretty nice. Got a real good staff of doctors. They're really decent. They'll back up a corpsman in almost any predicament he gets in to, and a corpsman's judgment is as good as gold, as far as the doctor's concerned. Really makes you feel good. I'm stationed right next to the Air Base and I think that's why we're getting most of our mortars and rockets in here. Trying to knock out some of the airplanes. I've been issued a .45 caliber pistol and I could have got an M-16 or an M-14 rifle, if I wanted to, but I wouldn't be using it that much, so I just decided to decline. A .45 is about all I can use over here. Anybody gets that close to me that I'll have to use my .45, I'll probably be too scared anyway. Probably have to pick it up and throw it at them, instead of shooting at them.

Boy, there are so many fights here between the Marines. They all go down to the club and they throw a few beers down and they really think they're hot stuff. The other night I was over there and this one guy in the corner was just getting really drunk. And all of a sudden he stood up and picked up a beer can full of beer, and took it and heaved it clear across the room and it bounced off the top of this other guy's head, you know. Never seen the guy probably before, and had no bitches with him or anything; he was just trying to start some trouble. Bunch of animals. (Laugh)

Marines over here treat the corpsmen just great, 'cause the way they figure it, if anything happens to us, you know, who's going to take care of them? They really respect the rate of the corpsmen. It really makes us feel good. We do as much as we can for them too.

Got a letter from a buddy of mine when I was stationed in Camp Pendleton. Just bought a new Triumph and he likes it real well. He's a Vietnam returnee. He was over here eight months and he got three Purple Hearts. Oh, by the way, three Purple Hearts will get you out of country, but I don't really want them all that bad, so I'll just stick out the whole 13 months.

Anyway, things are pretty much the same at Camp Pendleton. Kinda wish I was still there, but I volunteered for this place and I'm going to stick it out. I'm repeating myself, but it's not all that bad, but it's nothing compared to the stateside duty.

Well Pop, I know I got a lot of tape left, but I'm running out of words, so I'll close it off now and try to add a little bit more later ...

The last tape his father, Weldon Young came in December of 1968. I noticed a marked difference in the tone of his voice and attitude, as if he lived several lifetimes in those few short months.

A Corpsman's Legacy

Hiya Dad,

I got your package today and believe me, I can't tell you how good it was to hear your voice. I think that's just about the best Christmas present I could ask for. It's just so great. These taped letters are so much better than written letters. You can express yourself so much better. And as I say, it's just so great to hear your voice.

I'm not really good at thinking of things to say but, I've got a couple of these tapes and I'll see what I can conjure up in the category of saying something. I surprise myself every time I fill these tapes. It seems like I can talk all day long, but when it comes to thinking of something to say and putting it down on paper, it comes up as a different story. When I hear the voices on tape from the people at home, it's just ... I sit just here and imagine you all and what they were doing at the time of recording it. They're home and they're enjoying life and it kinda gives me a pickup, 'cause I know sooner or later I'll be out of this place and be home.

Well, I don't know what to tell you about Vietnam. It's an entirely different country. It's been war-stricken for so many years and these people are so tired of war and so undernourished and they have no provisions for the future. It's gonna take very many years to build up a half-way decent civilization around here. But we're over here to help them and I'm not bitter about being over here, because as you know, I volunteered to come over here. I'm glad I can help them in some way, but something else that makes me feel good is I know I'm helping my fellow man, fellow Americans.

I've seen some pretty bad stuff since I've been over here, but any time I can help, no matter how tired I am, or how depressed I am about the war, I just get in there and help just as much as I can. Just try to help save a life, stop the bleeding, or just save a limb or something. It's just a self-satisfying experience and I just can't express it in words.

Today's the 20th of December and we're supposed to get a big offensive. Well, it was supposed to start last night, but we didn't catch very much at all; just about normal. And tonight I can hear the flares popping up all around and I can hear bombs out on the other sides of the mountains and it's just hard to believe these people are at war 24 hours a day.

It's kind of a change after, what 19 years, I spent in the United States where it's a free country and it's peaceful, so to speak, compared to this place. And you come over here and you hear bombs going off and see flares in the air and you see rockets passing, mortars exploding and you see people getting hurt. And it's ... I don't know, you have to adapt to this kind of living and believe me, it sure doesn't take long.

I was kind of apprehensive when I first got over here because when I started seeing these men coming in with their legs blown off or arms or even their head or something like this. Maybe I'm ... nah, I was going to say maybe I've turned cold, but I don't think that's the word to describe it. I think it's, as I've said before, I've adapted to this kind of life. You see a man die, there's nothing you can do. You can't sit there and mope. You have to move on to the next man. And it may seem like

70

a morbid attitude to some people, but it's just like a job and after it's all over you sit back and think and worry about these people at home; the parents of the people that are being killed over here, but at the time it's just a job that needs to be done and it's a job I just feel fortunate I'm able to do.

The best feeling I've ever had in my life is saving another man's life. Knowing that you are the sole responsibility of letting this man live, you know. Your work, through your hands saved this man and - I don't know, when the man comes around and when he finds out there's one person that has saved him, it's a lifetime friend and it's something you just don't see every day. It's just a feeling you've never felt before.

A little bit on what I've been doing over here. I've been working here in the dispensary quite a bit. I've been going out on patrols - with the Security Marine patrols and I kind of enjoy that the best because, I don't know, sitting here in this place. You get people in here that are sick and it's a job that needs to be done, but I just don't feel like I'm using my capabilities to their fullest and when I go out and I'm able to help these men out there in the bush, it just really makes me feel good.

And every once in a while we go out on what we call MedCap patrols and we go out to the surrounding villages and help the people who are sick out there. I don't know - these people are so grateful for what they, the medical, can do for them over here. And whenever I'm going out with patrol on a MedCap, before we enter the village, the word spreads that bacsi is coming. Bacsi is the Vietnamese word for doctor. And every time I go out, I always bring a little bit of candy and pass it out to the kids afterwards and it's kinda good to see a smile on their face after, I'm sure, so many days of suffering.

As I've said before, there's supposed to be a big offensive and tonight we're in Condition One which is probable attack and I just kinda hope they forget about us, at least for tonight. Kinda slack on the sleep department and I'd like to catch a few hours, but can't convince Charlie of that, though.

Right now, I'm in DaNang, and I figure about, oh right after Christmas in January I hope sometime, I'll be able to move up to Quang Tri. And I've - now don't get mad, okay? I volunteered to fly Med Evacuation helicopters and I'm really looking forward to it. It's good experience, I guarantee it. But, it's a lot uh - I shouldn't say it's more dangerous, it just depends on where your helicopter goes. I know a couple guys up there at Quang Tri now and they just really enjoy flying and I'm just looking forward to it.

There is a shortage of corpsmen over here in Vietnam. It's almost getting down to a point now where it's drastic. They have a program over here that if, after your year over here, if you extend for six months, they'll send you on 30 days free leave anywhere in the free world you want to go. And I've been considering it; mainly because of the extra pay over here, and if I start flying I'll be getting flight pay. And I'll earn my wings, after 100 missions I believe it is, and that's extra pay right there.

As I say, there is a shortage on corpsmen over here and

*if I could do a job to help over here, I can't very well say
no. These Marines over here have so much respect for
us, it's really unbelievable. And I still am considering
this program. If I do extend, I'll probably come home for
30 days. It's a free leave; it's not counted against the
books. Probably stay home for 30, 35 days and come
back here for another six months. And at the end of six
months, I get another 30 days leave.*

*You know something that really makes me mad is, we
get this newspaper over here. It's called the Stars &
Stripes and I'm sure the newspapers at home are the
same way. Like two weeks ago, we got hit by Charlie
and they took Cam Lei Bridge which is about two miles
south of here. And they took and controlled that bridge
for most of the day before we were able to call air strikes
in and knock them out. But there were 150 Marines
around that bridge and 94 of them were killed and
something like 26 others were injured; I can't remember
the exact statistics. But when we got it back here in the
Stars & Stripes - the newspaper, it listed the personnel
as light casualties. And I'll tell you Pop, that's the
worst I've seen since I've been here and if that's light,
I'd hate to see heavy casualties.*

*I don't know - I know now because I'm over here but
the papers at home just don't tell the stories. It's so
built up on a political stand it's really pathetic. And
this bombing all sure hasn't helped things over here
and, as you said in a couple of letters before, you say it
was just a political move on Johnson and I'm more than
convinced that was the only reason we did it. And it's
just causing more deaths among the Marines and
Navy, Air Force - or anybody who is over here. And I*

just hope they get these things straightened out pretty quick.

Because, you know, another good example is that they're not supposed to be fighting in the DMZ zone, and boy, you should see all the casualties we get from up there.

Oh, hey looks like the end of this tape, so let me flip it on over and see what I can conjure up on the other side, hang on ... Okay, here we go. Well, five more days till Christmas. I really want to thank you for sending me that package and the salami before. It's just really great to get something from home. Tell you, it sure didn't take us long to finish that salami off. It tasted so good; just like being home almost.

I know it's gonna be kinda rough around here during the holidays but, I don't know, our spirits are pretty good. We kinda made a Christmas tree out of homemade decorations. Looks kinda funny but hope it serves the purpose. I just kinda hope I'm home for next Christmas and all the Christmases after that, but can't really tell. I just hope everybody at home enjoys the holidays and believe me, on Christmas Day, in fact all throughout this holiday period, my warm thoughts are all with you at home. I was pretty fortunate to be home last Christmas for the holiday time, and maybe not this Christmas but, as I say, watch out for next Christmas and the years to come.

I just can't wait to get out of the service and continue on with school. Right now I have my sights either continuing with medicine or going to dental school. I was talking to one of the doctors over here and he says there are all kinds of loans you can get and grants they give you to go to school. And I guess it's not too hard getting them. So I'm gonna try to make the best of it and if I don't decide to continue with a medical profession, I'm, in the back of my mind, still considering physical education.

As you know Pop, I've always been around sports all my life and I just really enjoy it. I'd like to become a coach someday. And maybe I can even have my own little Babe Ruth team, or something like that, to coach. Gosh, it doesn't seem like it's been four years since I played Babe Ruth. And I think that's one of those major things I miss while I'm here in the service is sports, not being able to compete against other people.

But I hope when I get in college I can play a little baseball or something. I played on this flag football team they have here. It wasn't very organized because of the monsoon weather and the rocket attacks. But we won six games and lost two and I was the quarterback and picked for the MAG-11 All-Star Team. We went over to Marine Headquarters Group on the other side of DaNang and played in a tournament and played against the different MAGs around MAG-36 from Chu Lai and MAG-39 from Quang Tri and MAG-16 from Phu Bai. And we fared pretty good. We came in third place.

I got my knee messed up, mashed up. I'll come home and say it's a war injury or something. (Laugh) But it was a lot of fun though, just to get out there and play and take our minds off this place. I couldn't think of a better way than sports. Unfortunately they have no facilities to make up a basketball court. We're thinking of just putting up a couple of hoops or something like that and shooting baskets. But there's no way we could make up any kind of team. Course there wasn't much of a football field. What we played on was kind of rocky and sandy and big dirt clods there, but it's something to get our minds off it.

Well, Pop, just want to take this time to wish you the happiest of holidays and have a great Christmas and a real good New Years. As I said before on the tape, I just want you to know I'll be thinking of all of you at home. And I think that's what keeps me going over here; it's just the image of you all at home. You're all safe and able to lead your free lives and I just can't wait to get back and partake in all the festivities, so I call it. I just hope you have the greatest Christmas that you had. I just know I'll be back, I hope, next year, to enjoy it with you.

Well, looks like the end of the tape's coming up, so I'd better cut it off. It was just real great hearing from you Pop and just say hi to everybody and sure would like to get another tape from you. Take care and I'll write as soon as I can. Thanks again for the packages and the tape and we'll see you pretty quick, I hope. Take care and love to all. I'll close it off now and try to add a little bit more later ...

To hear his hopes and dreams first-hand was the best way to get to know him and the greatest gift out of all the items Delbert gave me. I felt a connection and bond to my father even stronger than before. Many times I knew exactly what he was going to say, even before he said it. We laughed at the same places, felt sarcastic about the same things and it seemed very peculiar for me. But I had never felt more like his daughter than I did at that moment.

SHORTLY AFTER THIS, DURING ANOTHER VISIT with Delbert, he pulled out a large hard-backed certificate holder.

"This is the formal citation for the Purple Heart medal your father received," he said.

The certificate was awe-inspiring and formal in its blue leather cover with a gold seal stamped on the front.

"That is not the only medal Gary earned. He earned another one," he stated.

"He did? Can I see it?" I asked eagerly.

"Actually, we never received all of Gary's medals, just the Purple Heart. I tried for years to get them from the Navy with no luck. I finally gave up."

I questioned him more about the other medals, but it became too hard for him to talk about it. It seemed to break my grandfather's heart for his son to have given his life for his country and then not able to get his medals awarded in return.

After everything he unselfishly handed over to me, I wanted to figure out a way to give something back. I vowed then and there to somehow get those medals awarded. It had to be easier than what I had been through so far.

THE NEXT DAY I BEGAN MY QUEST FOR THE medals. I wasn't quite sure where to begin, but I searched on the internet and found an address for the Navy which looked appropriate. I wrote them asking for all information regarding my father, including every bit of information I could think of, including his service dates and service number.

A month later, I received a response from the Navy. Although it was a long letter, there was only one line that really mattered.

> *... A thorough search of records at this Headquarters has failed to locate any record responsive to your request ...*

I knew cutting through the red tape might be hard, but how on earth could they say no record existed? Not sure of what to do next, I continued to try to find new places to send my inquiries. Then, a couple of months later, I received yet another letter from the Navy, which I thought strange since their last letter seemed a dead-end. Again, it stated they did not have any records on Gary, however this time they listed an address to the Military Personnel Records center. So I sent off a letter to them requesting Gary's information.

I felt I *had* to accomplish this for my uncle and my grandfather. Remembering the look on Delbert's face, I knew I could not give up, no matter how long it took.

FIVE

I'D LIKE TO SAY THE SEARCH FOR SOMEONE WHO knew what happened to my father in Vietnam came as easily as finding his family, but that would be far from the truth. Many times I felt hopeless, but never more so than in 1997. Just weeks after I met Steve and Delbert, I was in a bad car accident. Not paying attention, a driver rear-ended me at almost 60mph causing whiplash in three areas and several broken bones. My life revolved around physical therapy, leaving me no time to actively continue searching, although I still hoped someone would find Gary's web page, or Jim's postings would uncover new contacts. But as months went by, my hopes waned.

More than a year later, the tides turned with an email from the sister of Ernest Bartolina.

To: *Stephanie Hanson*
From: *Jan Bartolina*
Date: *Tues, Apr 14, 1998 1:03pm*

I have just found your page on the internet. My brother, Captain Ernie Bartolina was a Marine med evac helicopter pilot in Nam. He too died on February

7th. I do not know if they were on the same plane. I am
trying to find out what unit etc he was in. Please email
me with anything you know and I will investigate more
too.

Do you know if Butch (Russell) Moke was co piloting
helicopter?? Sorry if this is rambling, but it is also hard
for me.

Maybe we can talk and find out more information for
each other. I would like that.

Jan

Her email filled me with excitement, since I was
positive the other families must have received more
information about the crash than mine. I sent back an
email to Jan confirming her brother and my father had
indeed been on the same helicopter.

To:	**Stephanie Hanson**
From:	*Jan Bartolina*
Date:	*Fri, Apr 17, 1998 12:01am*

I am so very glad you emailed me.

I have never tried to look up anything on the internet
about my brother, but for some reason on Easter I went
into a Vietnam helicopter chat room. I soon realized
that the last time I saw Ernie was on Easter – 30 years
earlier. I could not even remember the exact date he
died on. Someone in the chat room told me.

Another person in the chat room told me about the web

*site where I saw your name. When I went into the web
site I only looked at one name – your dad's. I saw he
died on the same day as Ernie. After reading what you
said on the site, I thought they were on same copter.
But you actually have more factual information than I
have. My mom probably has all that – I just have some
letters and stuff like that.*

*I think this is one of the biggest coincidences in my life.
I don't know why I looked for stuff about Ernie now or
why I just happened onto you. But I feel it is important
and want to talk with you and get to know you. I have
the name of the wing man on their flight. He tried to
get down to them – but felt all died instantly. He was
my brother's best friend. I'll send you a copy of that
letter if you want. I am trying to find him – maybe he
knew your dad.*

*Please continue to email also. I would like to share my
life with you and have you share yours too.*

Jan

My hopes plummeted with this email. Sorely
disappointed she and her family didn't have any more
information than me, I wondered how so many families
could have been left in the dark?

Instead of continuing to email back and forth, I called
her on the phone that evening. Jan feared I would blame
Ernie for my father's death, and I wanted to assure her
the thought never crossed my mind.

I also knew Jan felt bad she couldn't tell me more
about the helicopter crash. She promised to go through
the box of Ernie's things for anything helpful to me.

Although we didn't know it at the time, Ernie would play an extremely important part in my search.

One full tour in Vietnam was thirteen months. Ernie had been in Vietnam since April 24, 1968, almost ten full months, and formed many close friendships during that time. I later learned if I mentioned Ernie's name, rather than my father's name, people remembered more details about the crash. Without Ernie's vast popularity, I know my search very likely could have been over before it even began.

A FEW DAYS LATER A PACKAGE ARRIVED FROM Jan. She made photocopies of all the items she thought might be helpful to me.

The obituary on her brother appeared identical to the obituaries for my father and Russell Moke, the co-pilot.

Bismarck Marine Helicopter Pilot
Killed in Vietnam

A 26-year-old Bismarck Marine, Capt. Ernest E. Bartolina Jr., was killed in Vietnam Friday, when the helicopter he was piloting was struck by enemy small arms fire and crashed.

His plane was attacked as he was approaching a landing zone while on an emergency medical evacuation mission, and crashed seven miles north of An Hoa, Quang Nam Province.

He was the son of Mr. and Mrs. Ernest E. Bartolina, and was a graduate of Bismarck High School and the University of North Dakota.

Capt. Bartolina had been in Vietnam since April, 1968 and at the time of his death was stationed at the helicopter base at Marble Mountain, DaNang.

He had flown many missions and had been one of the eight pilots selected to transport the Bob Hope Troup on their recent tour there. He was assigned to Marine Air Wing I, Marine Air Group 16.

At the time of her husband's death, his wife, the former Sandra Jo Craig, was with her parents in Vienna where she is taking graduate work in language.

She is returning immediately to this country to make arrangements for his funeral. The rites will be held in Henryetta, Okla., with memorial services scheduled later in Bismarck.

Letter number one – of the four included – came from 1st Lieutenant Richard Hardin, the pilot of the chase bird. One of Ernie's best friends in Vietnam, he wrote to Ernie's parents just one month after the crash.

March 1969

Dear Mr. Bartolina,

The tragic death of your son, Ernie, was felt by us all here in 364 and especially by me personally. Ernie and I developed quite a friendship during the last year. We both lived in the same quarters at Phu Bai and here at Marble Mountain. We relaxed and spent most of our off duty hours together. Ernie was truly a person of strong character and his inspiration to me made my

task over here much easier. Ernie and I had many
things in common, especially our love of the outdoors
and hunting. Many hours we spent talking about our
past hunting experiences, his in the Dakotas and me in
Virginia. He had a fine love of nature and the wilds. He
often talked of his fishing trips to Canada. I promised
him if he would come and fish on the Shenandoah River
one summer with me, I would go to Canada with him. I
am sure I would have gotten the better deal in being
able to fish those many blue lakes up north.

Ernie and I often tried to fly together in the same
section and I was his wingman on the day of his crash.
We had flown about two hours of Med/Evac work when
we were called and diverted to an emergency pick-up.
Ernie was approaching the zone when he received heavy
enemy fire. He turned around and skated out and called
me and said his aircraft was hit and his flight boost was
going out. The flight boost is like power steering in a
way, but is absolutely essential for flight. Almost
immediately after he called his aircraft went
uncontrollable and crashed.

The impact was such, I am sure he was killed instantly.
I got to within 200 feet of the aircraft within seconds,
but received such intense fire and hits to my aircraft
that I was unable to land. I called for jets and Huey
gunships for coverage and I managed to get to the crash
with medical personnel on the third attempt. I later
talked to the Doctor and he said the six people killed,
died instantly. One man, a gunner, was by some
miracle thrown from the aircraft prior to the impact
and survived, but with severe injuries.

I hope this answers some of your questions and please feel free to contact me at any time if I can be of any assistance. Ernie's death was a tragic loss to you and for me. But we must keep our faith in God and press on with the difficulties of life ahead of us.

> *Sincerely,*
> *Dick Hardin*

Although I thought about the crash over and over during the last couple of years, this gave me my first visual image of what happened. I could see it, hear it. It made me think more about what the men went through in those last minutes. I'm sure they must have realized they were going to crash, although I couldn't imagine the horrific thoughts going through their minds.

But the piece of information that hit me the hardest was the mention of a possible survivor. I almost couldn't fathom the thought of this. Was it possible there was someone out there alive who had been with my father when he died? It seemed too much to hope for, especially since all accounts reported all on board being killed.

The second letter was from Dick's wife, Cheryl Hardin, with a newspaper clipping written about her husband.

"Conspicuous Gallantry" Nets Pilot Silver Star

A Marine helicopter pilot, who was awarded the Distinguished Flying Cross here in July, was presented the nation's third highest decoration for heroism during a ceremony here Oct. 1.

Capt. Richard P. Hardin, training officer for SOES, received the Silver Star Medal from Bgen. Robert F. Conley.

Capt. Hardin was cited for his "conspicuous gallantry and intrepidity in action," while serving with HMM-364, MAG-36, 1st MAW, in the Republic of Vietnam.

On the afternoon of Feb. 7, 1969, Capt. Hardin, a first lieutenant at the time, took off as wingman in a flight of two CH-46 transport helicopter. The mission involved the emergency medical evacuation of casualties for a unit heavily engaged with a hostile force in Quang Nam province.

Sustaining extensive battle damage when it came under intense enemy fire, the lead aircraft crashed in enemy controlled territory.

Setting the scene for Lt. Hardin's "conspicuous gallantry and intrepidity in action" was a heavy overcast and rain which severely limited visibility, and an extremely heavy volume of hostile small arms, automatic weapons and machine gun fire.

"Lt. Hardin," the citation relates, "fearlessly maneuvered his helicopter in an approach to the crash site. He approached the crash site to determine the fate of the crew."

He was forced to abort his first approach due to the intensity of the enemy fire. On his second approach to report the location of the helicopter, Lt. Hardin completely disregarded his own safety as he resolutely maneuvered his plane through the hail of hostile enemy fire.

When a friendly force reached the downed aircraft and reported the need for equipment to free a survivor pinned in the wreckage, Lt. Hardin is praised for proceeding to DaNang, embarking rescue equipment and personnel and quickly returning to the crash site.

When a Marine in the ground force was seriously wounded and required immediate removal, Lt. Hardin volunteered to re-enter the perilous area.

In this task, he is commended for "skillfully executing a high-speed approach through the intense hostile fire, landing in the dangerous area, embarking the injured man and departing for the nearest medical facility."

In addition to the silver Star and Distinguished Flying Cross, Capt. Hardin holds 37 air medals.

Now I had two references to a survivor. Should I believe the obituaries and newspaper reports, or these letters?

The other two letters were from Captain James Alton Cantrell, another pilot and friend of Ernie Bartolina. One was written the same month as the crash and had the same effect on me Dick Hardin's letter had.

February 1969

Dear Mr. and Mrs. Bartolina,

I know you have never heard of me, so let me introduce

myself. I am Capt. J.A. Cantrell and I have come through, roughly, the same duty stations, process of commission, flight training and eventual assignment to Vietnam as Ernie did.

I have had the pleasure of knowing Ernie some nine months prior to his death. Seven of those nine months Ernie and I were roommates first at Phu Bai and later at Marble Mountain. Ernie and I became very close personal friends immediately, partly I believe, because we had so much in common. The longer I knew him the more respect and admiration I had for him. There was a great deal about him that contributed to our very close friendship.

He came in country three months after me and as time passed and I made plane commander I asked specifically for Ernie to fly as my copilot on my first HAC mission. Later on as I made Section Leader and Ernie made HAC I asked again that Ernie fly as my wingman on my first Section Leader mission. He and I later flew many missions together this way and the teamwork we developed, and respect for each other's ability, added tremendously to our combat effectiveness, and to the personal satisfaction of getting a job well done. Ernie had an unbelievable amount of coolness, even under enemy fire, and for this I will always respect him. I am very sincere when I say Ernie had so much going for him; a gentle, pleasant personality, self-discipline, quick cool judgment, and at the same time he was a very skillful helicopter pilot.

I am still young and back home I have an 11-month old son, which I'm going home to see in a few days. Right now I can only imagine the tremendous loss you have both incurred. But I want you to know I have also suffered a great personal loss – one which strikes so deeply as to be beyond words.

But I can tell you too that Ernie died in a just cause and he is to be honored for the outstanding way he defended that cause and you can be exceptionally proud of the way you reared him. The principles I saw him stand for are no accident and I believe took a lot of effort from two God-fearing, patient, and conscientious parents. Through Ernie, I feel I know both of you very well and would like so much to meet you. I would like very much to be able to add some little consolation to your sorrow.

I'm sure you've been informed of the manner in which it happened. I feel the fact Ernie died trying to save the life of his fellow Marine is a great consolation in itself. I can think of no mission so satisfying as Medical Evacuation missions. Ernie was inbound to pick up an emergency med evac when the enemy fire caught both hydraulic boosts and with these gone, the aircraft was uncontrollable. This was only the second case I know of in the 13 months I've been here in which an aircraft had both boosts shot out. Only one man survived the ensuing crash. I do not believe Ernie suffered any. I'm sure he knew what was happening because he was still relaying his problem on the radio. At this point there was not a thing he could do but he was still calm and cool on the radio. Assistance was only seconds away and the enemy never reached his aircraft. I wish there were more I could tell you. I realize the deepness of your sorrow and I pray for you and the rest of the *family to accept the strength of God, who can and has, borne all our sorrow.*

I will be home in Pensacola around March 5th. I welcome you to call me collect if there is any additional information I can give you for consolation.

> *Very Sincerely,*
> *James A. Cantrell*

With now a third mention of a possible survivor, I felt a tiny flicker of hope come to life. Could there really be one? It was a lead I had to follow up on, no matter how slight the possibility may be.

So I set about searching for both of these pilots. I sent emails, posted messages and searched all over the internet, but to no avail. I could not find a single clue to the location of either pilot.

Years later, I eventually found Dick Hardin and spoke to him one time. But, I doubt I conveyed to him just how much his letters meant to me, nearly thirty years later. He had no idea when he wrote them, they would end up playing such a huge role in my journey.

SIX

IT'S OFTEN SAID ONE PERSON CAN MAKE A HUGE difference. Jim Fisher is one of those people. His first email started a chain reaction of events enormously impacting my journey.

> *To:* **Stephanie Hanson**
> *From:* **Jim Fisher**
> *Date:* **Sun, May 31, 1998 10:03am**

Stephanie:

Sorry Stephanie, I did not know your father personally, but we were in the same place at the same time, doing the same job, just with different squadrons.

I was a medevac corpsman with HMM-362 stationed at MAG-16 across the road basically from the DaNang hospital. It was called Marble Mountain and the air station where your dad and I flew out of.

Research tells me your father was likely flying with HMM-265, a CH-46 squadron and the only one I could find at MAG-16 in early 1969.

Best wishes. I hope you can locate someone who knew your father.

Former Medevac Corpsman
Jim Fisher

As I had learned more about Vietnam in the past two years, I realized I needed to conduct two different searches. After finding out Gary had only been stationed at MAG-16 for three or four days, I knew the chances of finding anyone who knew him from that time were probably nonexistent. To find those men, I would have to look for people stationed with him at MAG-11 in DaNang, thus my first search.

The second consisted of trying to learn what happened on the day he died, and this would come from the men in his unit who remembered the circumstances surrounding his death.

Although my father only got one flight, his interest and desire in becoming a medevac corpsman made me want to learn more about what kind of life he would have led, had he fulfilled that dream.

If Jim agreed to tell me more, I could get a first-hand view of a medevac corpsman's life in Vietnam and what my father longed to do.

I sent him an email, hoping against hope he wouldn't mind.

To:	**Stephanie Hanson**
From:	**Jim Fisher**
Date:	**Thurs, Jun 04, 1998 6:16am**

Stephanie ... As for HMM-265, men rotated in and out and the size of a squadron was probably about 120 -

*150 men. MAG-16 was an airbase across the road
basically from the DaNang Hospital and where most of
the corpsmen lived. It was just off the beach of the
South China Sea and a short distance from DaNang,
the Vietnamese city, China Beach, kind of an in-
country rest and relaxation area for service men, and
from Monkey Mountain, where armed forces radio and
television had a tower. It frequently took mortar and
rocket fire, as the enemy tried to get at the helicopters
and planes.*

*Marble Mountain was a piece of granite which
projected upward out of the ground and was truly out
of place as it sat on perfectly flat ground surrounding it
for miles. There was a small Vietnamese village at the
base of Marble Mountain and the natives carved
statues from the marble/granite and sold them to
servicemen.*

*If you get stuck and don't have any luck with what you
have so far, let me know and I will do what I can to help
you further.*

Good Luck!
Jim Fisher

Thankfully Jim didn't mind my questions and we
continued to correspond. One email contained a story I
would never forget.

Stephanie –
*You should be proud of your father. Volunteering to fly
medevacs in Viet Nam took a great deal of courage. The
VC (Viet Cong) and NVA (North Vietnamese Army)*

sometimes wounded our troops just to get a helicopter in a zone so they could try and shoot it down. There were bounties paid to them for certain people and machinery and downing helicopters was a big one.

At the base of Marble Mountain was a small village. Each week on the same day, two corpsmen, a doctor, a Vietnamese nurse and a Marine driver would go there in the morning to hold clinic.

My last time, we left at the normal time and arrived at the normal time. We went in what today would be described as a pick-up truck with a canvass topper.

In the middle of the village was a stucco building, like a village hall, with large stanchions out front. Inside we would see and treat patients for just about everything. We always finished about 11:30 in the morning and would be back at MAG-16 about noon.

This day we had an unusually large number of people to see and were running late. At about 11:45 a.m., a loud explosion occurred just outside our building. I thought it was a mortar attack and ran outside and stood behind a stanchion. I fully expected to look around it and see Viet Cong coming after us.

When I finally looked, our truck was blown to pieces and our Marine driver lying in the road with one of his hands gone.

Apparently some kids were playing around him and the truck and someone stuck a satchel charge between the cab and the back of the pick-up. I believe their thought was we would be almost back to the base and all would have been killed.

There was a Green Beret base near Marble Mountain and suddenly a tank rolled into the middle of the village. The Green Berets heard the explosion and came with a tank. We got the Marine evacuated and then got a ride back to the base.

I swear to this day the good people of that village knew this was going to happen and why they kept coming to the clinic, to keep us from leaving and being killed.

There are a lot of stories about Viet Nam. Most of them not so nice. Seeing that kind of horror every day or nearly every day, made you take immediate stock. After picking up my first serious casualties and KIAs, I made up my mind I wasn't going to it get to me. And that decision probably saved me a lot of grief.

I remember my first mission. We got a call to go into a hot zone, (where a fire fight was ongoing) and as we landed, I stooped down in the door of the helicopter and watched what I could only describe was a real John Wayne movie going on right in front of my eyes. Machine gun fire everywhere.

The crew chief, Frank Flagg, kicked me into the rear of the helicopter. I got up, looked at him with a dirty look and he said, "Let me tell you something, young man. If you want to stay alive over here, you stay out of that door."

When we got back to MAG-16, I was still a little miffed

*at Frank. I got my gear and started walking away from
the helicopter and Frank called me back. "Doc, come
here." I walked back and he pointed to a point just over
the door I had been crouched in. Three bullet holes, just
above the door. He said, "Those were put there while
you were in that door."*

*I never stood or crouched in that door again while in
Viet Nam.*

Jim Fisher

This was the real Vietnam, not just black and white
words in a schoolbook. Jim brought that country and the
war to life more than any class or dusty textbook ever
could.

But this was not the extent of the role Jim played in
my journey. He sent me links to other websites he
thought of value. One of these sites led me to a list of
FMF Corpsmen, basically a roster of corpsmen, but
without dates or locations of where the men had served.

At first, I just gave it a cursory glance, but then one
name lodged in my memory bank caught my eye – Dick
Olson.

I had received an email from a Dick Olson, many
months ago.

*I didn't know your dad, but I did attend the service held
in his memory at Marble Mountain. I arrived at
Marble Mountain on the day of his death and wound
up replacing him in the duty roster. It was a bad time
to be a corpsman. By the time I was evacuated in April,
we experienced almost 100% turnover due to injuries.
Dick Olson, former HM2*

This note had caused great excitement for me, but the email address corrupted in transit, leaving me with no method to respond. Could this be the same Dick Olson? I crossed my fingers and sent him an email.

To: **Stephanie Hanson**
From: **Dick Olson**
Date: **Tues, July 07, 1998 5:03am**

Yes, I sent you a message a number of months ago. I hope you have been successful in finding others that might have known your dad.

I forwarded your email address to a former corpsman who served at Marble Mountain and may have known your dad. I'm sure he would provide any info he might have. I've learned there was a lot of turnover among corpsmen during early 1969 at Marble Mountain and it's difficult to reconstruct an accurate chronology of events looking back through nearly 30 years of hazy memories. Do you know when your dad arrived in Vietnam? Do you have any information regarding which squadron he was attached to? If I'm not mistaken, in your original request for information, you said your dad was killed in early February and had not been at Marble Mountain very long. I arrived on February 7 or 8, 1969 and was evacuated after being wounded on April 19 or 20.

I tried so hard not to let my excitement get the best of me when I read Dick's email. I told myself repeatedly it was next to impossible someone would actually remember my father from those few days. But the very next day, one of my greatest wishes came true.

To: **Stephanie Hanson**
From: **Dick Olson**
Date: **Wed, July 08, 1998 5:02am**

Here is the info Mike Pepper provided me yesterday. Evidently your dad was killed on his first mission. Mike reports Walter Tyrrell (another corpsman) was "breaking in" your dad when things went bad. Mike will contact you shortly.

Communicating with you has made me reflect on the emotional conflict that arose around wanting to do my job and at the same time protect the interests of my family. I had two kids when I went to Vietnam. My son was born in May of '67 and my daughter in August of '68. I was pretty badly wounded in April of '69 and I remember thinking if I didn't make it, things were going to be very tough on my family. I'm leaving tomorrow for 10 days of trout fishing in British Columbia. I hope you learn everything there is to know about your dad. I'll talk to you when I get back.

And the next email came from Mike himself.

To: **Stephanie Hanson**
From: **Mike Pepper**
Date: **Wed, July 08, 1998 5:42am**

I hope Richard was able to pass on my information to you. I had been wounded in November, returned around January, flew awhile but had problems with grip, being wounded in the hand. I went to Wing and Gary went to Mag 16. I think he had been at the Wing Dispensary for a few months. (H&HS-1 or something like that.)

*Anyway, I believe it was his first flight on the 7th of Feb.
He was being broken in by Walter Ripley Tyrrell, an
HM-3. Both were killed in Arizona Territory, just south
and west of DaNang if I remember right. Feb and Apr
turned out to be a very bad time in Viet Nam.*

*I met Gary a few times. It's weird how your memory is
– we were all so young and full of it. We flew with
whatever unit drew Medevac. Normally no one wanted
it and they had to assign it to various pilots, rotating it
around. A few pilots who were Hot Dogs really liked
Medevac because it gave them a chance to REALLY fly.
They were Cowboys and loved the challenges.
Corpsman liked them too because you actually felt
safer, for some foolish reason, with them and they'd go
in where others wouldn't. Our goal was always to get
the wounded out. Our birds didn't have any armor to
speak of. We'd sit on a piece of 1" steel about 2' by 2'
and hope for the best. When we dropped in, the goal
was to get the wounded and git out quick. We took a lot
of fire and had only a 30 Cal on each side of the bird in
34's. They started using 46's about that time which had
more fire power, but no safer. Anyway, I have a
tendency to run off at the mouth. I'm really sorry you
didn't have a chance to know your Dad. The war
messed up a lot of lives.*

This time I let the tears come. I had really done it!
After more than 18 months of searching, I finally found
someone who remembered my father, no matter how
much or how little. It seemed so wonderful.

Obviously it was difficult for Mike to talk about these
old memories, so I wrote and tried to explain how his
recollections impacted me.

To: **Stephanie Hanson**
From: **Mike Pepper**
Date: **Wed, July 08, 1998 11:06am**

Thanks Stephanie. It does bring back memories that have been buried. Normally only the good times are remembered until something jars your brain. Then the rest comes in like a flood. I will dig through some of my "junk" for names. I'll see if I can find some names at Wing or Mag-11.

One I know of for sure is Murray L. Peters. One of the two best friends I have ever had. He was there when Gary was and would have known him better than me. I was in the hospital most of the time and Murray was not. Drop him a line, I'm sure he can help you even more than I can. I will look for what I have though.

Best to you and keep in touch. I'm glad you are pulling your early life history together. Hard to imagine what you have been through.

Best of Luck
Mike

The floodgates finally opened. Having gone months on end without finding anyone who could help me, I now discovered not just one, but two men who remembered my father.

That evening I called Murray Peters' home, and although Murray was not home, I chatted with his wife, Jennifer. She promised to talk to Murray about my call when he got home and have him get in touch with me.

To: **Stephanie Hanson**
From: **Murray Peters**
Date: **Tues, July 21, 1998 12:04am**

*Hi. I'm Murray Peters. HM3 in a past life, MAG 16,
1st MAW. I came into Nam in September '68, my
second tour. I was assigned to MAG 36 in Phu Bai
(just south of Quang Tri / Hue). We did some
Medevacs but mostly short range patrols and
ambushes. I really wanted to fly more so I requested
MAG 16. Just after Christmas I got my orders and
reported to DaNang at the end of January. Myself,
Dave Quigley, and Gary were the FNGs. We didn't
hang around the club, just sat out by the beach and
talked about what the missions were like and since I had
been in-country already, I was the "expert." I can't
remember specific conversations, just in general our
concerns about doing our jobs right, the high number of
casualties our medevacs were taking, and what a great
beach we got to live on. People transfer in and out every
day, bags get packed, moved in and moved out. Losing
two docs in one day was about as traumatic then as it is
now reliving the chief corpsman coming into the hootch
giving us the news and beginning to pack the sea bags.
I'm sorry I can't tell you much more – we were all so
young, and scared, and excited and each man
wondering to himself – how will I perform under fire.
Every day. And how many days you have left in-
country? I'm not doing this well, but then I don't go
here very often, all the guys I knew (our group suffered
50% WIA or KIA) and even seeing the names makes
the deaths feel all over again. I'll close for now. I'll see if
I have some pics. Don't think I had a camera then but
I'll look. Take care.*

I read these emails over and over, until I practically memorized them word-for-word. The actuality of finding what I had been looking for turned out to be far more rewarding than I hoped. One subsequent email from Dick Olson showed how writing to me was even harder than imagined.

To: **Stephanie Hanson**
From: **Dick Olson**
Date: **Wed, July 22, 1998 9:18am**

... I'm doing quite well now and rarely think about my old injuries. Sending that first email to you was an "iffy" thing. I'm still not sure exactly what prompted me. Gary's name stood out in my mind because I knew I replaced him on the flight schedule. Knowing I would be doing the same thing that got him killed was not a comforting thought.

We flew over the Gary's crash site on my first mission. As I recall, and this is hazy at best, their helicopter was hit by ground fire in the vicinity of Charlie Ridge just inland from An Hoa and headed for safety down the Hoi An river. We always went out that way after being hit, trying to get to a friendly area down at the mouth of the river. Apparently the helicopter was badly damaged and went out of control, crashing before it could reach the delta. I remember it was on the flat land area quite close to the river and not far from An Hoa. I remember thinking it must have been over very quickly. The fellow that broke me in on my first day pointed out a number of crash sites. It is possible I have confused them, but I don't think so. I was scared witless. Things like that tend to stay with you. I was concerned about

opening up something that should be left alone when I
responded to your request for information ...

All four of these corpsmen still communicate with me
regularly after all these years and I know their
unselfishness in putting aside their bad memories of
Vietnam in order to help me understand my father
would make Gary very proud. They all helped to heal
the hollow feeling that existed from the moment I found
out about my father.

And in a strange twist, the one who started it all, Jim
Fisher, turned out to have a connection with my search
after all.

To: **Stephanie Hanson**
From: **Jim Fisher**
Date: **Fri, July 24, 1998 3:08pm**

Walter Tyrrell and I were best friends. In fact Walt and
I planned to extend for six months in Viet Nam to take
advantage of an offer for a free trip to anywhere in the
world for 30 days. We were going to do it and go to
Europe and just bum around in Germany, France and
Italy for 30 days. We had to make our decision within
two weeks as to whether or not we were going to do it
and he was killed exactly two weeks before we had to
commit, apparently along with your dad.

Am very happy you have found your way around.
Believe anyone you contact would be more than willing
to help you. Best of luck.

Out of all the emails they sent to me, there was only
one term I didn't understand, so I called my brother to

ask what FNG stood for.

"Are you kidding?" Geoff chuckled.

"No, why? Why is that funny?"

"Because it stands for..." Geoff could hardly speak he laughed so hard. "It means Fucking New Guy."

Oh. I probably should have been able to figure that one out.

AMAZINGLY ENOUGH, I NEVER COULD FIND ANY corpsmen from MAG-11 that knew Gary. He served there for almost five months, but I had no luck even finding anyone from that timeframe. I also tried to find his boot camp buddies or those stationed with him in Camp Pendleton, as those would have been the closest friendships formed over the years. But, that search was even more impossible. I didn't have a clue where to start, when one of Jim Schueckler's postings on a message board came through for me again.

To: **Stephanie Hanson**
From: **Joe Hancock**
Date: **Tues, Dec 22, 1998 5:26pm**

I was stationed with a Gary Young at Naval Hospital Camp Pendleton from '67 till approximately Nov '68. I think he was assigned to HMM-164 operating out of China Beach or Marble Mountain and he was assigned to Medi-Vac choppers. If this is the same Gary, write back.

Even though Joe had the dates and the unit number wrong, I knew he meant my father, so I sent him a picture of Gary.

To: **Stephanie Hanson**
From: **Joe Hancock**
Date **Thurs, Dec 24, 1998 6:46am**

*Yes, it is the same Gary. I remember Gary as a very
nice guy everyone liked. I don't remember where he
worked on the wards at Campen (Camp Pendleton), but
the bunch of corpsmen and corpswomen were a real
tight group of people and we tried to do a lot together. I
guess deep down, we all knew where we were all headed
– to Nam. One trip a lot of the guys took stands out in
my memory. We decided to go up into the mountains to
Big Bear Lake and camp out. I rode on the back of a
motorcycle driven by Frank Redondo. It was my first
time on a large bike and the mountain curves were
scary for me. I remember Gary was on the trip and have
pictures of a lot of us. I haven't located them yet. I will
be off the next three days and will try to find them.
Rather hard looking for them, cause I have to go thru all
of them and there are a lot of memories there.*

*I arrived in Nam in Dec '68. In late January, I located
some of the Campen men and women at one of the large
hospitals near to Marble Mountain. I remember
visiting Gary 'cause their base was located right on the
beach and you could check out surf boards...I went out
on another operation and next time I made contact with
the group at the hospital, got the news of Gary.*

*Have you made contact with very many guys or girls
that knew Gary? I am trying to get the email address of
Chuck Bongers out in Wisconsin. I know Chuck
remembers Gary too, but he may not reply. You have to
understand Stephanie, this was all real hard on all of*

*us, especially when it was a friend. In the nature of
what we had to do over there, death was something we
had to face every day (sometimes 20 times) and going
back and opening up old memories is tough. I really
debated whether to answer, but realize you are trying to
get to know your father. I don't think I have helped you
much, unless I can find the pictures at Big Bear. If I do,
I will mail them to you.*

To me, the word unselfish perfectly describes these
men. It would have been so easy to either ignore the
postings they saw, or to delete the emails I sent. But
even knowing what painful memories it would bring
back, they made the decision to help me.

I could understand their hesitation, especially since
prior to writing me they had no idea I grew up never
knowing my father. I'm sure they thought I heard
endless stories about him all my life. It wasn't until I told
them the whole story they learned what a huge gift it
was for me to hear from them. Then they felt they
couldn't do enough.

To: Stephanie Hanson
From: Joe Hancock
Date: Mon, Dec 28, 1998 3:30pm

*Stephanie, to be like your father is a wonderful
character trait. Gary was very good looking, very
courteous and the type of guy I would have not had any
problem taking home to meet my sister (even though
she would have been four years older than him). It was
very tough on us to hear about him getting killed. I had
forgotten about him crashing on his first flight, but
remembered it after you wrote about it. I always looked*

*forward in getting away from my outfit and seeking out
some of the gang from Campen. The good part of it was
the fellowship we had. The sad part was they always
knew who had gotten killed since we last visited. I will
eventually hook up with some of the ole Campen gang
and tell them you want to "talk to them."*

Not long afterwards, I heard from the other
corpsman.

To: ***Stephanie Hanson***
From: ***Chuck Bongers***
Date: *Wed, Jan 06, 1999 8:04pm*

Dear Stephanie:

*I heard from Joe Hancock in Fairfield, Texas yesterday
and he told me you are Gary Young's daughter. Gary
was also my good friend while at Naval Hospital, Camp
Pendleton after I came back from Vietnam. He was
always a real special guy and we used to hang around a
lot. We went camping at Big Bear Lake with a bunch of
guys and I believe I have a few pictures I can send.*

*I was so sorry to hear about your Father and there is
not a week that goes by I don't say a prayer for him.
That's 30 years. Anyway, I'm anxious to hear from
you, answer any questions you have, and try and find
the pictures for you. Take care of yourself. Your
persistence is something Gary would be proud of.*

Regards,

Chuck Bongers

Thirty years of prayers. What a wonderful testament to just how terrific a guy my father must have been. Soon I received a package from Chuck with reprints of pictures. I ripped it open with barely contained excitement.

Five pictures tumbled out and I laid them out side by side. Two of the pictures were of Gary alone. Taken in 1968, he had grown up a lot since his high school picture and I marveled that the older he got, the more I looked like him. One picture was of a group of guys in their room in the barracks and one showed them in the Enlisted Men's Club. But my favorite picture was of Gary and a fellow corpsman named Bill Prewitt taken down in Tijuana. Gary had this big grin on his face. From the dates on the back of the pictures I saw they were all taken just a couple of weeks before Gary shipped out to Vietnam. Obviously his one last hurrah state-side.

One other facet of my father's life came to light in the form of a nickname.

> To: *Stephanie Hanson*
> From: *Chuck Bongers*
> Date: *Sun, Jan 24, 1999 8:42am*

Stephanie, glad to hear you got the pictures and glad you like them. As far as any nickname for Gary, the only one that jumped out for me was a name that many called him at Camp Pendleton, but was unique to our little group. And that was "Harry Pung." It made absolutely no sense but was a good endearing term because he had a great sense of humor and it seemed to fit. He never was upset by it.

Will stay in touch with you and hope you with me.

Harry Pung? A lot of the times the nicknames I heard were self-explanatory, but this one stumped me. And no one else seemed to know either.

However, several months after this, I received a packet of letters Gary sent to a high school friend during his time at Camp Pendleton. In one of those letters, I found the story of this nickname. Gary teased Bill Prewitt that anyone whose last name started with a 'p' was a "dumb shit" in his exact words. So, of course, Bill put a 'p' in front of Gary's last name and called him "Pung." The others in the group decided to change "Gary" to "Harry" and the rest was history.

SEVEN

JIM FISHER PLAYED SUCH A HUGE ROLE IN THE early stages of my journey, it was almost impossible to think he could find more to contribute. But he provided one more crucial piece of the puzzle.

To: **Stephanie Hanson**
From: **Jim Fisher**
Date: **Sun, May 31, 1998 10:03am**

Have you tried www.popasmoke.com? This is an internet listing for all of the helicopter squadron associations from the Viet Nam era.

There will be a meeting this coming September in Pensacola, Florida of all of these helicopter squadron members from Viet Nam. I am sure your dad's squadron members will be there.

I found two people attached to that squadron. Does not mean they knew your father, nor even in-country when your father was. Just means they are the persons to contact regarding that squadron. It is likely they have members who might remember your father, although he was very new to this squadron and it has been nearly thirty years.

I wish you luck. The two names are Sam Kelly and Bruce Lake and their phone numbers are attached.

They can tell you about the upcoming reunion in Pensacola as well ...

"Pop A Smoke" is the website for the USMC / Vietnam Helicopter Association and proved to be the most valuable tool I found. Formed in 1988, the group started by a few friends gathering together for a reunion and eventually grew into a full-fledged association with over 5,000 members by the time I found them. The entry page to their website explained it all.

USMC / Vietnam Helicopter Association
Pop A Smoke

"When a Marine in Vietnam is wounded, surrounded, hungry, low on ammunition or water, he looks to the sky. He knows the choppers are coming..."
Leonard F. Chapman General
USMC Commandant of the Marine Corps

During the Vietnam War from 1962 to 1975, helicopter crews were able to locate their fellow Marines on the ground by asking them to "pop a smoke" in the landing zone. The brightly colored smoke grenade identified the ground unit and landing zone and provided wind information to the pilot. Today, we are reuniting those individuals on the ground with the individuals who flew as flight crew on those missions. We are asking

them to Pop A Smoke so we can find each other.
Through our organization's newsletter, and now the
Internet, we establish and maintain contact with all
former Marine helicopter pilots, crewchiefs, gunners,
corpsmen, flight surgeons, chaplains, maintenance and
other support personnel.

Every two years we get together in a different part of
the country and have a reunion in a new LZ. Our
numbers are growing rapidly, and we're glad you
found us.

Semper Fi

I felt so reassured to find a group who actively supported people's searches to locate others. This statement finally gave me the courage to make my first phone call.

Sam Kelly, the reunion leader for HMM-265, was one of the two names Jim sent me from my father's unit. With my nerves on edge, I picked up the phone and dialed his number, even though I realized the low odds of this person knowing what happened to my father. Although no one answered, I continued to call a few more times with no success.

Then, afraid I would lose my nerve if I waited another day, I decided to call Bruce Lake, the other squadron member. On the second ring, a woman answered the phone.

"Is Bruce Lake available?" I asked nervously.

"No, he's not," she said. "This is his wife. May I ask who's calling?"

I'm sure she wondered why an unknown female called to talk to her husband.

"My name is Stephanie and my father was killed in Vietnam. I believe he belonged to your husband's unit and I hoped he might talk to me about Vietnam."

"I'm sure he would be more than happy to talk to you," she said warmly. "However, he's not home right now. He should be back in about an hour though, and I can have him call you."

Knowing they lived in New Hampshire, I offered to call him back. "I don't want to make him call long-distance," I said.

She insisted on taking my number and promised to let Bruce know I would call and we said good-bye.

I couldn't handle the thought of sitting around idly, so I left and ran some errands. Within an hour I arrived back home, and a message from Bruce blinked on my machine. I called him back immediately and he picked up the phone on the first ring.

"Is this Bruce?" I asked.

"Yes, are you Stephanie?"

"That's me. I hope you don't mind, but I wondered if you would talk to me about your time in Vietnam?"

"My wife explained," Bruce said kindly. "What would you like to know?"

I briefly explained about my adoption and the little information I uncovered so far. "I know Gary was at Marble Mountain in February of 1969."

"Well, that's when I was there. I was a helicopter pilot for HMM-265."

"Do you remember your unit's helicopter accident on February 7, 1969?"

"I remember it well. But I don't recall Gary's name."

I tried to think of other clues to help prompt his memory. "I know Ernie Bartolina was the pilot of the helicopter."

"That name doesn't ring a bell either, which is strange because I knew almost every pilot from HMM-265."

"Well, I think Ernie was with HMM-364," I said in confusion.

"Those are two separate and completely different units. Corpsmen, such as your dad, did not have their own unit designation, but were assigned to fly with a different unit each day. Any unit number attached to Gary's name would have been the unit he died with."

"Does that mean Gary wasn't flying with Ernie?" I asked.

"I have several Vietnam databases here at home. Let me do some searching and call you back in a little bit."

After we hung up, I sat there blinking back tears. Gary wasn't on Ernie's helicopter? If it turned out to be true, I would lose my connection with Jan and I didn't want that to happen. It would also mean the letters from Dick Hardin and James Cantrell were not about my father's crash. Had all I learned been wrong?

Ten minutes later Bruce called back. "Okay, there were two helicopters lost that day from two different units, HMM-265 *and* HMM-364. I remember the crash from my unit very well. John Prombo was the pilot and a very good friend of mine. In fact, I was very close to two of the men lost that day."

"The name Prombo sounds familiar to me, but I didn't know why," I said. "Maybe it's on some of the paperwork I have."

"What do you have?" he asked.

I grabbed my stack of papers and flipped through the different items, describing each one to Bruce.

"You have the memorial service program?" Bruce asked, startled. "What are the other names listed?"

I read him the other five names.

"Each squadron held their own memorial services," Bruce said. "It's highly unlikely Gary died in the HMM-265 helicopter, but was included in the memorial service with the men from HMM-364."

"So Gary might have been with Ernie after all?" I asked hopefully.

"Well, it's getting confusing now. I know our bird crashed into the water. Do you know anything about Gary's crash?"

"Yes," I said excitedly. "I do know it crashed on land and not water."

"From those two pieces of information, I think Gary must have been flying with HMM-364, and somewhere down the line the unit number got mixed up. I suggest you return to the Pop A Smoke website and look up the reunion leaders for HMM-364," Bruce said. "Hopefully they can help you further."

"I can't thank you enough for what you've done for me," I said. "This is a huge discovery and explains the difficulty I met when trying to find out information on my father. For the last two years, I had the unit number wrong."

Bruce promised to make copies of the information and send it in the mail to me.

AS PROMISED, A FEW DAYS LATER I RECEIVED HIS letter.

Dear Stephanie,

I commend you for your search efforts and wish you every success. I hope I did not confuse you with my

*comments in our telephone conversation, but this is
what I can only assume from the facts you shared and
the information I have:*

*Because your father was listed on your memorial sheet,
I must assume he was on the HMM-364 aircraft and
not on our aircraft. Usually each squadron held their
own memorial services and it would be very unlikely
Gary would have gone down on our HMM-265 aircraft
that night and been listed on the information you have.
I don't have all the details, of course, but it was my
understanding there were only four crew members on
the HMM-265 aircraft that went down. One survived
by swimming to shore and the other three did not
survive. Your call has helped me learn that the name of
the other crew-member on our aircraft was GySgt.
Wallace C. Bergstrom.*

*The confusing part to me (see the photocopy I've
enclosed) is that the first five names listed on 02/07/69
show the aircraft type as a CH-46A. I could be wrong,
but it was my understanding our squadron was the
only squadron with all the "A" model H-46's. The
other squadrons could usually lift a little more because
they had the newer "D" models with a slightly bigger
engine and a few other modifications. I know the CH-
46A information is correct for Glover, Prombo and
Bergstrom because they were in 265 and I qualified
them to fly. I'm guessing the CH-46A data for Tyrrell
and your father may be in error.*

*From the research you've done so far, you can see it is
sometimes difficult to piece these things all together so
many years after the fact — even for those who came*

116

*back. The photocopied page is from the Vietnam
Helicopters Pilots Association directory. Until two
years ago their data was only about pilots. Recently
they decided it was just as important to research and
document data about air crew members who served and
died beside the pilots. I'm glad they have started to
include that information in their database.*

*I sincerely hope the little bit of information I provided
has helped you fit together a few more pieces of the
puzzle. As I said on the phone, I give you lots and lots
of credit for seeing this through. You are a very special
person for doing so. When you serve in combat with
someone it builds a bond that is difficult to understand
unless you have been through it.*

*One of the pilots I trained with through every phase of
training was Jeff Rainaud. He died in a mid-air
collision. Jeff and I had military ID numbers only one
digit apart — that's how close we were in training. We
always competed with each other. There were times we
disagreed with each other and other times we got along
well, but we always had fun trying to outdo each other.
I still feel he cut short his leave before going to
Vietnam, just so he could get over there before I did! I
will never know how he felt about my flying, but I had
the greatest respect for his flying ability. It is still
difficult for me to deal with his death. At least I finally
stopped seeing him in my dreams every few nights
when I finally touched his name on The Wall. One
thing I feel ashamed about is I have not been able to
contact his family. I tried a couple times but kept
running into dead ends and was never sure if I could
handle it well if I did reach them. So, now you know*

why I feel so proud of you for having the strength, courage and persistence to keep researching and finding out all you can about your father — because I have not found the strength necessary to deal with finding Jeff's relatives. You've continued through a process that certainly must have been difficult for you at times — researching the family connections and making the contacts, etc. — and you continue your search. It takes a special person to do that and I wish you every success!

If you found me in Pop A Smoke then you should be able to easily look up the names of those who served in HMM-364 and look for those who served in 1968 and 1969. By contacting them, perhaps you can learn more about your father.

By the way, I'm sure you know everyone had the greatest respect for Corpsmen. Some carried weapons and some did not, but they all responded to the call for "Corpsman" whenever and wherever they were needed. Many, many times we lowered a Corpsman down into a "hot" area on the hoist cable so he could treat the wounded Marines and hook them onto the cable in a stretcher. (Often the injuries were in areas where we could not land, that's why we used the cable.) The Corpsman would stay in the jungle until we lowered the cable back down to pull him out. I have the greatest respect for the courage of men like your father. Many, many men owe their lives to people like Gary Young.

Thank you for your call and best of luck. Don't hesitate to contact me if you think there is any other way I can help.

The enclosed piece of paper contained information from the Vietnam Helicopter Pilot Association book with February 7th highlighted.

Tyrrell, Walter R.		*CH-46A*
Young, Gary N.		*CH-46A*
Glover, Raymond E.	*HMM-265*	*CH-46A*
Prombo, John A.	*HMM-265*	*CH-46A*
Bergstrom, Wallace C.	*HMM-265*	*CH-46A*
Bartolina, Ernest E.		
Moke, Russell, E.		
Miller, Charles W.		
Shank, Rodney G.		

This was the same book Jim Schueckler used in 1996 to determine Gary's unit number and it's very easy to see where the mistake happened. Since Gary and Walter were listed as flying in a CH-46A, everyone assumed they were also in HMM-265 with Glover, Prombo and Bergstrom. One little mistake caused so much confusion.

HMM-364 STANDS FOR MARINE MEDIUM HELICOPTER Squadron 364, also nicknamed *The Purple Foxes*. The Purple Foxes have a spirit and mystique that distinguishes them from other Marine helicopter units. It didn't take long for me to learn how fortunate I was my father got assigned to the Purple Foxes that day.

The Pop A Smoke website listed Walt Wise as their squadron reunion leader and I gave him a call. But his time in Vietnam came after my father and he didn't remember Gary or the incident of February 7th, 1969, but looked through his data then suggested, "Why don't you call Gene Brady, the Commanding Officer of HMM-

364 for that time period. He was also one of the most popular COs in Vietnam and that is saying a lot, because many of the COs were intensely disliked."

So on July 6th, 1998 I made the phone call which would change my life.

Colonel Gene Brady flew jets before commanding a helicopter squadron. Assuming command on February 2, 1969, he became the epitome of the Purple Fox spirit and was dearly loved by all his men. An outstanding Marine decorated with several medals, he received the Purple Heart, the Silver Star, and our Nation's second highest decoration for heroism – the Navy Cross.

Had I known all this about Colonel Brady, I doubt I could have ever summoned up the courage to call him directly. But, I will be forever thankful for my ignorance, which let me dial the phone once more. His wife, Ginny, answered and I asked to speak with her husband.

A moment later, a man picked up the phone and barked, "Gene Brady."

I wasn't sure how to begin and stumbled a bit to get my words out. "I was wondering if I may ask you some questions about your time as Commanding Officer of the Purple Foxes in Vietnam in 1969?"

"Which news affiliation are you with?" he asked gruffly.

News affiliation? Was he used to being interviewed by the media? Not sure how to answer, I finally replied, "Just me, sir."

He must have heard the nervousness in my voice and spoke more gently. "What would you like to know?"

"My father was a corpsman killed in a helicopter crash in Vietnam. I think he was flying with your unit and Walt Wise suggested I call you." I gave him a quick synopsis of my story and what I knew about the crash.

"Unfortunately I took over the squadron at the beginning of February 1969," Gene said. "I do slightly recall the crash. And I remember Gary's name, but only because I gave a tribute at the memorial service for the men we lost."

"Yes, I saw your name on the program," I replied.

"I remember Ernie Bartolina and Russell Moke, but not any of the others. However, I still keep in touch with many from that time and I'll call around to try and find out more information for you, if you'd like. I am attending the reunion in Florida in September and I will see if I can dig anything up there, too."

"I don't want to be a bother," I said hesitatingly.

"Stephanie, you are now a member of the Purple Fox family," he replied. "We accept you as one of our own, which is the least we can do after the sacrifice Gary made for us. You will always have a place in our family."

Choking back tears, I couldn't speak.

"Don't worry, Stephanie. We'll find something out," Gene said gently. "I promise you."

FONDLY KNOWN AS PAPA FOX AND MAMA FOX, Gene and Ginny Brady truly became family to me – they call me their daughter-in-love. Having them in my corner is one of the greatest assets I could have. When Colonel Brady calls, everyone answers and they all help as they can.

They say behind every great man is a great woman, and in Gene Brady's case, I believe it. Ginny Brady is one of the strongest, warmest and most thoughtful women I have ever known. She raised six children, much of the time by herself, when Gene was deployed. I know there were many difficult times in her life, and yet, she still managed to inject humor into it all.

One time, talking to her about being a "single" parent, she related this story to me.

> As for coping while Gene was CO of HMM-364 in Vietnam, it was "one day at a time." We had six teenagers with all the usual problems: chauffeuring, homework, laundry, chaperoning, and a couple of trips to juvenile hall for "curfew violation."

> I remember one amusing experience: while cleaning the boy's bathroom I found an ominous-looking capsule that was purple and orange and immediately thought DRUGS! I tasted it to see if it had a bitter painkiller taste, which it didn't. So I sat them all down in the living room after school, showed them the capsule, where I found it, and I wanted some answers. "Oh, Mother, that's the dog's worm medicine!" our 16-year old son said.

Any time I listen to someone talking about Gene Brady, one of his pilots *or* enlisted men, they fairly glow with pride and joy, knowing they were part of a very special time in HMM-364's history.

One such pilot, 1st Lieutenant Chuck Story, wrote this short story about Gene Brady, also known as the Skipper.

Courage Tempered By Compassion

> In April of 1969, while assigned to HMM-364 at Marble Mountain, I flew medevac chase on the wing of Lt. Col. Gene Brady when we received a call for an

emergency medevac located southwest of An Hoa fire base. Upon arrival and receiving a zone brief, the Skipper advised the ground troops there would be a delay while awaiting gun-birds to offer cover while effecting the medevac.

The radioman, almost in tears and with total disregard to radio discipline, pleaded for an immediate evacuation of his wounded Marines. The Skipper replied to this request as if he were the father of a troubled son, comforting and assuring him we would render the necessary assistance to bring the mission to a successful conclusion. Due to not knowing how long gun-bird assistance would take, the Skipper advised he would attempt the medevac without the benefit of gun coverage, asking me to provide the "tremendous" firepower of a single .50 cal. machine gun on board the CH-46 (the crew also threw rocks).

As he made the descent into the zone, the tree lines lit up like Christmas trees; I followed him to about 300 ft. with the starboard gun firing and suddenly it quit. Now, we were a gun-bird without a gun.

I yelled for the crew to fire and began climbing back to altitude. It was then I learned my right gunner had been hit. The Skipper was pinned in the zone by small arms fire when the ground forces reported tube pops of mortar rounds. I again rolled in to provide a measure of cover fire for his exit from the zone and we returned to base without further incident.

Later, the Skipper and I visited the wounded gunner in the hospital. This visit was as much for me as the

*wounded crewman. The manner in which Lt. Col.
Brady spoke and the comfort he offered, not so much in
words, but the tears, touches and the look in his eye,
said it was okay. We did the deed and saved a Marine.*

*The kind of raw courage demonstrated by the Skipper,
tempered by his compassionate manner in dealing with
young men facing terror and/or death was burned into
my memory forever. I will take that with me proudly
wherever I go.*

Gene always continues to think of the men who
served under him, and it is just one of the reasons he still
commands great respect. Twenty-five years after
Vietnam, Gene commissioned a special watch for the
men who served under him. On the faceplate is the
cartoon caricature of the Purple Fox – Swifty himself.
Having a Purple Fox watch signifies you are part of
"The Brady Bunch" and is something to be very proud
of indeed.

Shortly after I spoke with Gene for the first time, I
received a package in the mail from him. Inside was one
of my most cherished possessions – my very own Purple
Fox watch.

EIGHT

IF MY JOURNEY WERE CAPTURED IN A PHRASE, I would call it *Random Acts of Kindness*. The reason I found any success in my search can be attributed to countless strangers coming forward to offer their help. And by random, I mean those people who did not know my father, or anything about his crash. In a quest like mine, you would think only those who had information for me would come forward. That's certainly what I thought, but I couldn't have been more wrong. My search truly showed me the inherent generosity of the human spirit.

Speaking to Gene Brady, combined with the discovery my father flew with HMM-364, rekindled my enthusiasm to approach anyone to see if they knew my father. Since email seemed to be the best method to communicate, I worked up a standard request, incorporating all the new information I found.

I am looking for people who knew my father. His name was Gary N. Young and he served as a Navy Corpsman. From the information I have so far, he arrived in Vietnam in September of 1968 and served at the Marine Corps Hospital at Marble Mountain in the DaNang area for MAG-11. At the end of January in

1969 he was then assigned to MAG-16 to fly medevacs. Shortly after, on 2/7/69, Gary was with unit HMM-364, and the CH-46 helicopter he was crewing was shot down while on a Med-Evac mission in Quang Nam province. All seven aboard (except one possible survivor) were killed in Arizona Territory, just south and west of DaNang. The pilot of that chopper was Ernie Bartolina Jr.

I know it can help to see a picture to jog a memory. I have a picture of Gary on the Virtual Wall.

If you knew him or had any ideas on where to find men who did, I would appreciate the help.

Thank you.
Stephanie

Although I felt more confident now than before, I still cautiously wondered how strangers would react to my reaching out for help. So I first went to the FMF Corpsman member list where I found Dick Olson and chose several corpsmen to send my email. I sent out eleven emails and thought of it as a test run.

I knew it was unlikely any of these eleven men would turn out to know my father, but I hoped maybe one or two of them would respond.

Incredibly, almost every single person I wrote to answered back almost immediately. None of them knew my father, but they still felt the need to answer. Many of them responded with just a brief note, but they were all so positive, such as ... *I wish I could do more*, or *I regret I can be of no further service*, and even *I would have been proud to serve with him*. Some of them went further.

From Clark 'Doc' Fritze: ... Sorry, but I didn't know your father; I was gone by the time he arrived in-country. I hope you are able to find the information you are seeking and I am very sorry for your loss. I am sure your Dad is looking out for you and smiling down on you. It took a special man to serve with the Marines and even a more dedicated man to fly medevacs. I hope your search is successful.

From Robert 'Doc' Dirr: ... I commend you on your quest to gather information about your father. Unfortunately, he and I were in the Navy during different time spans (I was discharged from the service before he even got to Vietnam). You are headed in the right direction, dear. Keep surfing those military web sites, and sooner or later, sometime and somewhere, you'll get a positive reply. I sincerely wish you good luck, and I certainly wish I could help you.

But...know this: if your father volunteered to go from a relatively secure area like a hospital base, in order to go where the action is to help his fellow Marines, than he was one hell of a good man. The next time I'm at The Wall, I'll be sure to stop by his panel and say a prayer.

Thanks for contacting me. Sorry I couldn't help you out.

From Paul 'Doc' Blakely: ... I was a Corpsman with a Marine Battalion and we got heroic support for my wounded from HMM-364 and the great and heroic Corpsmen who flew the Medevac missions. I even had my life saved by the brave men in the helicopters. I can

say without having known him he had to have been a
brave man. Corpsmen are a breed apart from other
military people and we grieve for each other. I hope you
are successful and I will be asking the people I know
from that year. Keep me informed on your search.

These responses touched and surprised me immensely. Before I started this search, my preconceived notion of a Vietnam veteran was based on the Hollywood and media myth that most veterans were drugged-out, whacked-out, and quite possibly homeless, non-contributors to society. It sounds horrible to put it down on paper that way, however, the sad truth is I had no idea.

Many of the corpsmen wrote to tell me they passed along my inquiry to other fellow corpsmen and Marines they knew. A number of them sent me names of those they thought might know my father. And, some of them gave me new websites and associations to check.

One of these websites called "The Few" had a guest book where Marines could leave messages. I used its search engine function and sent out more emails to anyone who served in Vietnam during February of 1969.

Once again, I immediately received responses, but this time most of the answers came from men who served in ground units, known as the grunts. This meant there really wasn't any possibility of knowing my father, but regardless of where they were from or who they served with, the responses all had the same flavor.

From Harry Johnston: ... *Stephanie...... These guys*
were great. I was alpha co. radio operator from 68-69
and they would come in the thick of fire to help our
wounded and though I didn't know your father you

must know what he did was the highest as looked upon by the Grunts. The helicopter pilot that would fly through intense fire, and come to our aid of wounded in battle meant everything to us! They always came when we called! SEMPER FIDELIS

From Paul Sterling: *... I've been trying to remember things from thirty years ago that might help your search and/or bring you some comfort. I arrived in Vietnam several months after your father was killed, so my words and memories can only help you visually.*

DaNang was a pretty city on the coast and Marble Mountain was a base nearby. It wasn't really a mountain, as the area was mostly flat near the coast. I was there only briefly, but recall the area was always under assault.

China Beach was east of DaNang and had one of the longest beaches I've seen. Again, a beautiful place-except for the war! It ran north from the city.

With regard to your father, without sounding patronizing, please let me share with you my thoughts on Corpsman in general: it's hard on anyone in battle with a rifle in hand! Can you imagine how it must feel to be next to a soldier with a weapon, with only a medical pouch!?

I trust your father had the same attributes I saw in almost every corpsman I met; courage and compassion. Good luck on your search.

From Charlie Mitchell: ... *Good search, hon... wish I could have helped. I'll say the Navy Corpsmen were (still are) a SPECIAL breed of servicemen. Not to sound too hammy, but a Marine can't live w/o them.*

From Roy Elliott: ... *Stephanie, I doubt I knew your father as I was in a Huey unit (gunships) that flew support. I was there from Dec. 66 to Aug. 68.*

You may have heard it many times but let me say it again. The corpsman did more, with less, for The Few then anyone else "in-country." Many gave their lives tending to others. "Semper Fi" is allowed to a chosen few - your father is one. Contact me if I can be of any assistance.

From Jim Rocha: ... *Stephanie, I just wanted to say how sorry I am about your Dad. I can only imagine the heartache you and your family have experienced over the intervening years.*

As a Navy combat veteran who served in Vietnam twice in the late 60s, I know now how blessed I am to have survived. I thank God every day for my deliverance from that place and for giving me a loving wife and son. I don't say this to make you feel worse, just to underline I DO appreciate every day of life.

I didn't know your dad, but I knew many corpsmen along the way. As a whole, they were some of the most dedicated and self-sacrificing folks I ever knew. And, despite the usual rivalries between sailors and marines,

*I doubt you'll find any Marine grunt who served in
Viet that would have anything negative to say about
their "docs."*

*Many (too many) corpsmen paid with their lives. Over
and over again, they placed themselves in extreme
danger to save the wounded, while the enemy targeted
them specifically. Proof of their courage and devotion
can be found by looking at the "honor roll" of corpsmen
who received Medals of Honor, Navy Crosses, and
Silver Stars, many of these posthumously. At the same
time, many other corpsmen who put it on the line every
single day were never recognized for their sacrifice.*

*So Stephanie, your dad is in very good company. Those
of us who survived know we must honor the memory of
every sailor, marine, flier, and soldier who didn't
return alive. So, your dad lives on in all of us, and he
will never be forgotten. I honor him for his sacrifice.*

These emails showed me just how much Marines
loved their corpsmen. I mean *really* loved them. Email
after email came in proving this fact.

AROUND THIS TIME POP A SMOKE ADDED AN
outstanding feature on to their website. They put up a
list of all their members who had email addresses –
almost 1,400 of them. In addition to the alphabetical
listing, their list contained unit numbers. HMM-364 had
a couple of hundred men listed, and some included their
service year.

I chose a few for 1969, hoping they might have been
in-country during the month of February. Again, in less

than an hour, I received responses. One of these responses changed my search forever.

To: **Stephanie Hanson**
From: **Willy Williams**
Date: **Sat, Aug 1, 1998 3:40pm**

Stephanie,

Thanks for contacting me in your attempt to get or find help. You are headed in the right direction. The Pop A Smoke site is one of the best I have seen for HMM-364. I am very sorry I do not have any information that might help you in your search. My humble suggestion is you mass email the HMM-364 Pop A Smoke members in hopes of getting more info from them. They are having a reunion in Florida soon and the sooner you get the email out, if you haven't already done so, hopefully the better your chances.

Good luck in finding the answers to your questions. If I can be of any further assistance feel free to email me again, and if you do get your questions answered, I would like to know that also. I will continue to use the limited resource and contact with the veterans in an attempt to help you locate the info.

Semper Fi
Anchors Aweigh
Willy

The thought of sending out a mass email had crossed my mind, but I wasn't comfortable with the idea until Willy suggested it. I wrote back to Willy asking if he really meant it. He again wrote and encouraged me to do so, and with his "permission," I decided to go for it. It took me a couple of days, but I sent out an email to every Purple Fox on the list.

On the very first day I received emails and they kept pouring in, and in and in. The responses came at the rate of ten to fifteen a day, some by email and soon some through regular mail.

From Dick Clifton: ... I'm truly sorry about your father and wish I had some information for you. My time with the "Purple Foxes" was in '66 flying the UH-34. However, in January of '69, I was flying OV-10s with VMO-2 out of Marble Mountain and was very familiar with the Arizona Territory. It was not a friendly place.

Reading your letter was not done without emotion. It took me many years to gather the courage to visit the "Wall." But when Popasmoke had a reunion in D.C. in '92, we visited en masse. Not a dry eye in the crowd.

Although corpsmen were officially sailors, in our units they were Marines and had the respect of every man.

Best of luck in your quest. Semper Fi.

From Bob Wiegand: ... I served with HMM-364 in 1967 and 1968. The squadron was based at Phu Bai in the north. We were never based at Marble Mountain during my tenure in Vietnam, although periodically, we would send small detachments to operate from DaNang or Marble Mountain for short support operations. I was medevaced from Phu Bai in June of 1968 and spent four months at the Naval Hospital at Camp Pendleton, Ca.

I never knew your father nor am I acquainted with any details concerning his last mission in Arizona Territory.

I wish you well in acquiring more information. As you know by now, there isn't a Marine pilot or crewmember alive who doesn't hold Navy corpsmen in the highest esteem. Every one of us who served in the worst fighting of that unfortunate conflict has personal stories about the truly incredible bravery exhibited by our "Docs."

Your father certainly sounds like he fits the mold. I would have been proud to have had the opportunity to serve with him. Best of luck to you and your family.

From John Braddon: *... I served in Nam in 64 with HMM 364 and would have no knowledge of events in 1968. But if your dad was a Navy Corpsman serving with Marine helo squadrons, he was a hero. Our Corpsmen were magnificent. We all owe these dedicated brave men a great debt of gratitude for the heroic service they rendered in saving the lives of others.*

From Dave (Pretzel) Bilbrey: *... I was in 364 during my 2nd tour. At the time your father got shot down I was serving with 263 at Mag 16. I, and for that matter all Marines, have the greatest respect and love for all Navy Corpsmen. I have worked with many "Docs" on the countless medevac missions I flew. There is a* *possibility I may have met your father but, in all honesty I can not remember if I did, my memory of that time is mostly a fog.*

I wish to extend my belated and heartfelt condolences and wish to tell you I knew the kind of man your father was. I witnessed the numerous, and often untold bravery, dedication, and commitment all Navy Corpsmen showed while performing their duty. This was not done for country, Navy, or unit. They did this because there was a wounded Marine that needed help, and they did this often great risk to themselves. I wish you luck in finding what information you can, somebody out there knows.

From Larry Britton: *... Stephanie, I had just joined HMM-364 at the time. I knew Ernie Bartolina and Dick Hardin, but only in passing. Unfortunately I don't have any information that might help you in your search.*

The Navy Corpsmen who flew medevac with us were some of the bravest, most unselfish men I have ever known. Even if you aren't able to find out any more information on your father, you can take pride in knowing he was one of the Navy's finest. Best wishes in your search.

From Dennis Welsh: *... I wish I could help you in your quest. I didn't arrive in Vietnam until June 69. I just recently joined this organization and am having to constantly jog my memory. I hadn't thought much about Nam until recently. I wish you the best of luck in* *your endeavor. As a gunner on medevac missions I always had the utmost respect for the corpsmen who flew with us and especially those who paid the ultimate price.*

If at all possible, let me know how this turns out.

From Warren Smith: *... I served with HMM 364 from when it was first formed and in Vietnam with them in the early part of 1964. I didn't know your Dad but can tell you the Marines hold the Navy Corpsmen in the highest regard. They would go willingly to care for us under all the worst conditions. Knowing they were behind us allowed Marines to go forward with less fear. God bless your Dad, he is with the warriors that loved him.*

From Steve Shupp: *... First let me tell you I didn't know your father. He was in-country after I came home from my first tour. While I was with HMM-364 I was a mechanic and crew chief and when we flew Medevacs, the most important person in that helicopter was the corpsman.*

I think the corpsman in Vietnam had one of the most difficult jobs. Most of the corpsman we knew we just called them "Doc." I can assure you your father was well respected and liked by everyone. Corpsmen were just very special people.

Stephanie, I have read your letter over and over and I wish there was something I could tell you that you need to hear, but I can't. I do feel so very sorry for you and I know there is someone out there that can help you with this chapter of your life.

Hang in there kid. Your Father would be very proud of you. And Stephanie, you should be very proud of him...

From Al Chancey: *... Dear Stephanie, I commend you for your efforts to learn about your father. My Vietnam tour ended in May 1968, when I was shot and wounded while flying a Medevac mission in HMM-364. So I did not have the opportunity to serve with your father, and I'm sure that was my loss.*

However, having flown as a pilot on many Medevac missions with a Navy Corpsman as part of my crew, I think I can tell you something about your father. From the picture I can see he was a handsome, cheerful and outgoing young man who enjoyed life to the fullest. I know he was a man of great courage and compassion, for he volunteered to fly Medevac missions with a helo squadron when he could have chosen to remain in a safer assignment. I know he was totally dedicated to doing his job and doing it to the very best of his ability, for that was the mark of every Corpsman I ever served with. And when his best efforts at preserving life proved unsuccessful, as they sometimes did, I know his pain and anguish were intense. It is certain Gary Young had a deeper understanding of what is good in humanity than most do, for while everyone around him was involved in the madness of destruction, he was solely devoted to preserving life. Finally he is the father of a loving daughter, and from across the years he has inspired her to seek understanding. What greater legacy can a father have?

The Marines are respected throughout the world as a proud, close-knit, professional organization. They tolerate, but seldom fully accept outsiders in their units. The rare exception is the Navy Corpsman. Because he has consistently proven himself worthy, the Corpsman is accepted as a part of the Marine brotherhood when he serves in a Marine fighting unit. This is the respect accorded Navy Corpsmen by Marines. This is the esteem in which Gary Young was held by men of one of the world's most honored fighting organizations.

Your father, like so many other young men in the history of this great country, gave his life in the cause of freedom. The fact that the Vietnam war was not a popular war nor one easily understood does not render his sacrifice any less noble. You can be so very proud of him, for he gave his all, not in selfish pursuits, but out of devotion to his fellow man. The friends I lost in Vietnam are held in a very special place in my heart. The name of Gary Young now resides with them, for the memories of such men deserve to be honored and preserved in the hearts of others.

I wish you success in your search and peace and understanding in life. Semper Fi.

Who would have ever thought these men, stereotyped as crusty, old codgers, to put it lightly, would write so compassionately? Although the quantity of the responses took me by surprise at first, I finally realized the overwhelming response happened because my father was a corpsman. The respect and love these men had for their "docs" now transferred to me.

ANOTHER RECURRING THEME IN THESE EMAILS showed how all Marines respected the Purple Fox unit. Everybody seemed to know of the Purple Foxes.

From Delmar Crawford: ... I was late in the war and just eighteen when I got there. MAG16 included all the helicopter squadrons assigned to Marble Mountain at that time which included HMM-364. Their nickname and radio call sign was 'Purple Fox.' It was and is hard to go in any men's room in the far east and not see that logo stenciled over the facilities. They were and are the most bonded of all Marine Corps squadrons...

From Daryl Riersgard: ... I did not know your father because I did not get to Viet Nam until 1970. There is something special about the "Purple Foxes." This may be hard to explain to you. This particular squadron (HMM-364) already had an extraordinary reputation well before I got there. The reputation was such that we all requested to be assigned to this squadron when we arrived in DaNang (for our new combat assignment). We had to draw straws when the seven guys checked in.

Two of us were lucky and we got assigned as we wished. I truly believe we flew longer, tried harder and had more spirit than the rest (not that there was anything wrong with any of those other squadrons). Our Purple Fox logo on the tail of the helo said GIVE A SHIT. That meant we

*did give a shit and thus we did try harder to rescue our
fellow Marines who were in trouble. After awhile, the big
bosses (Commanding General) decided it was not proper
to have this logo, so we changed it to G.A.S (like no one
could figure that out).*

*Like your dad, we were the crazy, gung ho, young men
who decided to do something for our country. It was
patriotism and a lot more. We were the hard-charging
guys who wanted to be in the middle of the action. As
such, we ended up with the finest bunch of Marine
pilots you could imagine...fun-loving, free-spirited,
loyal guys. We were loyal to a cause and to a special
'band of brothers.'*

*We fought in an unpopular war, but then 5 or 10 years
ago, it all of a sudden became okay to be part of the Viet
Nam experience. We could talk about it, we could share
our stories and we could admit to the world it was us
who laid our lives on the line. This is why this POP-A-
SMOKE group is so special. This was part of the
healing I spoke about earlier. Yes, we are all still
healing, you and me and thousands of other people
affected by the war.*

*If I can fill in any other details about anything, please
let me know. God bless you because you are special and
because you care enough to put this history together.*

The Purple Foxes are truly an exceptional group. If
you were to look at their personal email addresses, the
great majority of them have references to their time with
this unit. Addresses include variations on phrases such
as *purplefox*, *364*, *CH-46*, and *Swifty*. Over 30 years later,

these men still have great pride in knowing they served with this squadron. This group of men would go to any lengths to help find my answers.

THE HARD WORK POP A SMOKE PUT INTO THEIR association and website shaped a huge part of my success. Their board listed five men, so I wrote to each one with my sincerest thanks. I received answers from all of them and one of them contained a very pleasant surprise.

> *To: Stephanie Hanson*
> *From: Roger Herman*
> *Date: Wed, Aug 26, 1998 10:24am*
>
> *Stephanie,*
>
> *Thanks for the very nice note. I write the newsletter for the Association and I will publish your letter in the next issue. I'm glad we were able to help you out after all this time.*
>
> *FYI, our membership rules allow relatives of those deceased USMC aircrewmen who were killed in Vietnam to join our organization in the names of their loved ones. If you are interested, please feel free to fill out our "FNG" join-up form on the website.*
>
> *Semper Fi,*
> *Roger Herman*

Interested would be an understatement. I logged on to the site immediately and within minutes I printed out all the necessary paperwork. In one week, I received a large envelope in the mail from Pop A Smoke. The smaller envelope inside was labeled with just three big letters.

FNG.

I was officially a Fucking New Guy.

SHORTLY AFTER THIS, THE WEBMASTER OF POP A Smoke also sent me an email. Although just a couple of sentences long, those few words packed a big punch.

> *To:*   *Stephanie Hanson*
> *From:* *Wally Beddoe*
> *Date:* *Tues, Sept 1, 1998 9:19am*
>
> *Stephanie,*
>
> *I just mailed your request for information to about 1,400 Marine Helicopter personnel from Vietnam. Hopefully you will get a response.*
>
> *Best Regards!*
> *Wally Beddoe*

1,400 men? With the type of response from the couple of hundred letters I sent out, you can imagine the kind of results Wally's email brought in.

> **From Jim Erwin: ...** *Stephanie: I'm really sorry about your dad — there were a lot of fine men who didn't come back — but I'm sure you've heard that before — like a lot of other guys who flew in Viet Nam, I was one of them — I was in HMM-164 at MM (Marble*

142

Mountain) — I didn't know your dad but I know what type of person he must have been — aside from all the macho stuff, he really cared for people thus his work — — belief in what he was doing but most of all love for his country and his family — and knowing there was real danger was willing to lay down his life trying to help others — Stephanie, thanks for having a dad like him — I know he'd be proud of you too, trying to find someone who knew him — best of luck in your search — I would have been proud to have served with him.

From Steve Sunderman: *... Hi Stephanie. Regarding your father: we moved north in September '68 to Phu Bai. I was a '46 pilot with HMM-265 working out of Marble Mountain most of my tour but I missed your dad's tour. Let me add something: I take my hat off to the Navy corpsmen who served with our Marine units in the field. Many of us owe our lives to their incredible bravery and devotion to help shot-up Marines in the field. These were the darkest days of the war for helicopter crews and those troops who rode the choppers. Good luck, Stephanie and may God be with you.*

From Randy Crew: *... Stephanie—I didn't get to Vietnam until July of 1969, so I didn't know your father. I have a feeling someone in our Pop-A-Smoke organization will be able to help you however. HMM-364 was an outstanding squadron. Good people.*

I just wanted to say, as a former Marine helicopter pilot, Navy corpsmen are on the top of my "Who I Respect the Most" list. I never met one who wasn't loved by the Marines he took care of. Corpsmen were special.

I did want to tell you this one personal experience I had with Corpsmen. In August, 1969, I was flying co-pilot on a UH-1E "Huey gunship." We finished all the morning missions they had for us that day and were shut down at Vandergrift Combat Base near the DMZ to wait for more missions. Sitting on the edge of the cabin of the Huey eating C-rations, I looked up to see two huge, mud-caked Marines and one small baggy Marine approaching us. The biggest of the Marines stopped in front of me and said in a commanding voice, "Sir, our Doc wants to see your helicopter."

I looked at the smallest Marine, who had a sheepish smile on his face, and noticed the Navy Corpsmen insignia on the front of his Marine cover. "Sure," I said, and stood up to show him the guns and rockets and other features. As the Doc and I walked around the Huey, the big guys followed closely behind. It was as if they wanted to make sure their Doc got to see all he wanted to see and was treated with proper respect.

When the tour finished, the Doc thanked me, the big guys thanked me, and I watched them return to their platoon of Marines resting in the tall grass beside the helicopter area. Sitting back down to my canned peaches, I shook my head and smiled at the memory of the tone of voice used by the biggest Marine. He did not want to disappoint his Doc. If the Doc wanted to see the helicopter then, by God, the Doc was going to see the helicopter and no Lieutenant was going to stand in the way. That memory still gives me a chuckle. Those guys loved their Doc.

All those young men were special, Stephanie, but Corpsmen were extra special. Good luck. I know your Dad would be proud. Hope you hear something soon.

Semper Fi.

Rarely did an email not cause me to shed a tear or two. The sheer number of responses was extraordinary enough, but the depth of emotion in them astounded me. My father loved being a corpsman and taking care of his Marines. I know he would have been proud to know his Marines were now taking care of his daughter.

NINE

LOOKING BACK, IT IS ALARMING TO REALIZE JUST how close I came to ending my search before it even really began. Prior to the emails coming in fast and furious, the limited contact I made with the veterans revealed just how much pain still remained from the Vietnam War.

It's easy to understand. Over 58,000 men killed in Vietnam and all servicemen shared one emotion regarding these deaths – a combination of fear, revulsion and absolute horror, with no time for the mind to adjust to this kind of trauma. The day after attending memorial services for their fallen comrades, it was business as usual. The only mechanism many had to handle this emotion was to bury it. And unfortunately, due to the unpopularity of the Vietnam War, these emotions have remained buried and unhealed in many veterans for over thirty years.

With my search, I knew I opened up some of these old wounds, and I feared it might be too much for some of the men, such as O.C. Baker's email highlighted.

To: **Stephanie Hanson**
From: **O.C. Baker**
Date: **Wed, Aug 05, 1998 7:50pm**

Dear Stephanie, I apologize for not answering your email immediately. Your request touched my heart and brought back some very deeply felt and aching memories. It has taken me some time to compose myself and to prepare a reply.

I am sorry I did not know your father. With a caring daughter like you, it is obvious he was a caring man himself and his character and legacy lives on in you. I believe you are searching for information that will help you understand your heritage from him and enable you to accept your situation. That act of searching is a tribute to both of you. I am sure he would be proud of you.

I can't provide any specifics on your father, but what I can do is provide some information about the environment he lived in during his final days. Perhaps knowing what he and his fellow flight crewmen did will give you a sense of his accomplishments and of his commitment to the Marines he was trained to save.

I was the aircraft maintenance officer of HMM-364 "The Purple Foxes" from the fall of 1968 until the spring of 1969 when I became the squadron operations officer. Initially we were at Phu Bai and then we moved to Marble Mountain.

I knew Ernie Bartolina, but not nearly as well as I wanted to because our time together was very short. He was very soft-spoken and one of the most gentle and composed persons I have ever met. His eyes revealed a combination of knowledge, acceptance and determination that generated immediate confidence in him, a confidence that was not misplaced because he was one of the most respected pilots in the squadron. I tell you this about Ernie because I want you to know your father did not die because he was flying with a weak or inexperienced pilot on that final mission.

Time has mercifully dimmed many of the details and facts of those days, but I recall our discussions of how Ernie persisted in attempting to accomplish this mission despite bad weather. People said he attempted to get to the Marines on the ground by having them talk to him on the radio and guide him based on the sound of his helicopter. A very hazardous procedure, but one Ernie must have felt necessary given the circumstances. The crew truly sacrificed their lives in an attempt to save a fellow Marine.

I will pass your request on to some other Purple Foxes of that time in the hope they may add some information. It would be very unlikely for pilots to have much contact with your father because of the way the medevac crews were assigned and in the CH-46 the pilots are sort of isolated up front, and their main contact with the rest of the crew is only with the crew chief over the aircraft intercom.

I should also point out no one could be ordered to fly. Every flight crewmember, including your father, had to specifically volunteer and request to be placed in a flight status.

Maybe someday your story will help people realize and remember when our country called us to arms, rightly or wrongly, there were thousands of people who answered that call and those who perished are still dearly missed and mourned by all of us survivors.

May God bless you Stephanie,
Owen C. Baker

O.C.'s recollections of Ernie Bartolina and his memories about those final days meant more to me than he realized. O.C. didn't know I talked to Ernie's sister and what he wrote was a gift for me to pass along to her. Because Jan harbored an unfounded fear I would blame her brother for my father's death, I knew this wonderful testament about Ernie would be of great comfort.

After I forwarded his email to Jan, I also sent O.C. a reply, explaining my relationship with her. I hoped it would provide a small source of comfort in return for causing him such pain in having to remember that awful day.

THIS PAIN ALSO BECAME EVIDENT THE FIRST TIME I spoke with Lance Corporal Norm Dare. He knew Ernie Bartolina who personally nicknamed Norm "Iowa" in reference to Norm's hometown.

In our initial conversation, I wasn't sure what to say, so I let Norm do the majority of the talking.

"I was there with HMM-364 the night your father died. I was sleeping in my hootch and they woke me up to go help deal with the aftermath. I faintly remember your dad, although I only knew him as Doc," his voice choked with emotion. "It was such an awful blow to lose this crew. I haven't spoken about this to anyone in twenty-nine years. I hate to remember it." He kept starting to speak, but then stopped as he broke down.

I found it hard for me to keep my own emotions in check, and didn't want to intrude on his recollections, but thought maybe it would be easier for him to answer questions from me. "Do you remember if there was a survivor?"

"I'm not sure," he answered. "I remember having to help write the letters to the families. It was one of the most awful things I had to do over in Vietnam. I have some of the paperwork still in my attic and I can look for it and contact you later in the week."

"I would really appreciate that," I replied. "But I'm so sorry to do this to you."

"It's okay. But maybe we should continue via email," Norm said. "It might be easier for me to write instead of talk about it."

"That's perfectly fine with me. Whatever is best for you," I said.

We said good-bye and when I hung up the phone, I put my head down on my arms and started sobbing. For the first time I had connected with someone who knew my father outside of email, and while difficult to see the emotions in their writings, to hear it first-hand devastated me.

That evening I lay in bed thinking about the phone call. After replaying our conversation in my head over and over, and recalling all the pain I read in the emails, I finally determined this was the end. I would do no more searching and be happy with what I discovered. The closer I got to the people who were there, the more emotional it got. I decided I couldn't stand to put them through this just to satisfy my curiosity and to pack it all up and count my blessings.

However, the next day, Norm surprised me with an email. I thought I might never hear from him again, let alone so soon.

To: **Stephanie Hanson**
From: **Norm Dare**
Date: **Sat, Aug 08, 1998 12:03am**

Steph,

I found my list tonight – couldn't sleep. Ernie Bartolina, 1stLt Russell E. Moke Jr., Cpl Charles W. Miller Jr., and LCpl Rodney G. Shank were the Marines that died with your dad. There were usually five Marines on a medevac mission, two pilots, two gunners and the crew chief, so there must have been a survivor. I remember going back to my hootch and just settled on the cot when I had to go back to the squadron hanger. They were killed in the afternoon and we worked all night and into the next day typing letters and sending information to Headquarters in D.C. All I can really remember about the crew was that we all called your dad DOC, and Ernie's smile. I had barely turned 18 when I shipped out to Vietnam, naive as hell and scared to death. Guys like Ernie helped us FNGs get accustomed to the shit we had to endure. No one liked to get to know the new guys for fear of befriending someone and then watch them die, or like in your father's case see them leave and never see them again.

The nightmares are still real but I can still see most of their faces. I can still remember the shock on the faces of most people the day your father died. It was my first blood. I knew the Marines and had seen your father on several occasions. The Navy corpsmen were our angels of mercy. They saved more lives than they will ever get credit for. When we would pick up the wounded, especially in a hot LZ, as soon as we got off the ground the corpsmen would be all over the wounded like stink on shit. I remember times when we would have to leave our guns to help hold compresses on the bleeders. In any case you can rest assured it happened quick and with little pain. Will talk to you next week.

Respectfully, Norm

I felt a little better after I read Norm's email. I knew it was difficult for him, but he tried his best to give me what information he had.

That evening he called again. Although he hadn't slept much over the last couple of days, he sounded much better and reminisced a little about Vietnam.

"So were medevacs really the most dangerous type of flight?" I asked at one point.

"Absolutely. And the most vulnerable moment was during take-off after they loaded up with the injured. The helicopter would tilt forward and wait to get the RPMs up to take flight. We were like sitting ducks for the enemies," Norm paused. "I have a few more men I can try to find to get some more information for you."

"I don't know how I will ever be able to thank you for what you have done for me," I said gratefully. I knew I didn't want to continue my search, but I wasn't going to stop Norm from trying to help. Not after all the pain I caused him.

"If I can get one smile out of that damn war, it will be worth it."

This statement tore at me. It seemed my search accomplished both bad and good. But which one outweighed the other? I remained in a quandary over it all, then I received two emails in a row that helped make up my mind.

> *To:*   *Stephanie Hanson*
> *From:*   *John Baker*
> *Date:*   *Thurs, Aug 13, 1998 12:04am*

Dear Stephanie,

I am truly sorry for the loss of your father and the loss of his presence in your life. Be assured he was a brave young man who possessed all of the traits I am sure he has passed on to you. You too are brave because it takes great courage to face that which makes us grieve, but by facing it we overcome our doubts and fears.

Thanks for writing me, because as a corpsman I worked on many young brave men, like your father, who died and I am sure left many relatives in the same situation as you. I have always wished I could contact them, and tell them how brave their "son," "father," or "brother" was facing such a terrible frightening situation each day in Vietnam.

That someone was with them when they died. That they were held close, and loved by all of us who worked to save them. That they called out for those they loved, and we answered their desperate calls. It still makes me so sad to think of these young men dying at such a young age when they had their whole lives ahead of them.

So, what I am saying is you've finally given me a chance to say to someone the things I haven't been able to say for over thirty years. You have helped me overcome the grief I have had for over thirty years. For that I will be eternally grateful.

Stephanie, I will write again if I have any info for you. Thanks again for helping me face my fears and helping me overcome them.

You, like your dad, have a great deal of courage.

Semper Fi
John "Doc" Baker

The first veteran to tell me point-blank my search helped him and John's email made me think. Some good *could* come out of my search, but was it enough?

Then, later that day, came the deciding email for me...

To: **Stephanie Hanson**
From: **O.C. Baker**
Date: **Thurs, Aug 13, 1998 5:13pm**

Dear Stephanie. It is my turn to thank you for passing my email on to Ernie Bartolina's sister Jan.

When Ernie died I was determined to tell his family what a great person he was, how much he was respected, and how deeply sorry I was at his loss. But somehow I just never was able to follow through. I had some belief that such a communication would only add to their grief and I could never put the words together. That bothered me, and I really felt for all these years I

*somehow failed in a very important responsibility I had
to both Ernie and his family. Your passing my email on
to Jan has greatly eased that long time burden.*

*The history of your birth and adoption and subsequent
discoveries of your heritage are most heartfelt. As I
indicated I have passed on your search request to some
other "Purple Foxes" of that time. In particular I talked
to Courtney Payne, my assistant aircraft maintenance
officer. Courtney is one of the finest persons and best
Marines that ever donned the uniform. He has some
specific information and potential additional contacts
relating to your search. He will be in contact with you
shortly, if not already. I will let Courtney and
subsequent contacts respond to your questions rather
than relay them second-hand.*

*Please let me know if I can be of help to you in the
future.*

*Semper Fi
O.C.*

After speaking with Norm and receiving these two
emails, I couldn't deny it. The story of my father and my
journey to get to know him seemed to provide a unique
and profound sense of healing to more people than I
would have ever thought. While it may be painful at
times, for some odd reason my search helped other
people. I knew now I should continue my search with a
much clearer conscience. I wasn't sure why my story
held so much power for these guys, but I finally felt like
I gave a little something back to those who helped me
out so much.

By opening up to me and sharing stories of their time in Vietnam, many never shared before, a catharsis occurred, allowing many to expose their pain for the first time and therefore begin an emotional healing about a time that shaped their lives forever.

TEN

THE FIERCE LOYALTY AND COMMITMENT MARINES have for each other is exemplified in their unwritten rule of *Leave No Man Behind*. In every case possible, they are absolutely unwilling to leave one of their wounded or killed brothers in enemy territory. Medevac missions occurred almost every day in Vietnam, and sadly many of them were followed by recovery missions.

The Purple Foxes established their own Recovery Team, like many other Marine CH-46 squadrons, due to the intense tempo of operations. 1st Lieutenant Courtney Payne, the Purple Fox Maintenance Control Officer, led some recoveries in 1968 and all the recoveries during the spring of 1969. While I searched for the details of my father's crash, I hadn't given any thought to the events that took place during the recovery. One phone call changed that.

"Hello, Stephanie!" a booming voice said. "My name is Courtney Payne. O.C. Baker gave me your name."

Courtney was full of life and brimming with confidence, and from the moment I heard his voice, I instantly felt a connection with him.

"Hello! Yes, O.C. said you'd contact me," I replied.

"I worked for Major Baker in Vietnam as the

Maintenance Control Officer and head of the Helicopter Recovery Team for HMM-364. The recovery team's job was to repair or recover helicopters after they had battle damage and were down," he explained. "My team recovered your father's body and the other members of the crew."

"Oh," I gulped, at a loss for words.

"Would you like to hear what happened?" he asked gently.

"Please, as much as you remember."

"Our team got called out shortly after the helicopter was shot down. It crashed into a rice paddy near an old French graveyard. When we went out to try and get to the aircraft, we came under intense enemy fire. We took cover behind the gravestones until the infantry units and air support could hold off the enemy long enough for us to reach the aircraft. By the time we got there, all were dead."

"But I heard a rumor there was one survivor."

"I hadn't heard of a survivor. But Dick Hardin, the wingman, landed before we got there. It's possible he took out a survivor."

"I've been looking for Dick Hardin. There is still so much I don't know."

"I don't recall Gary, but I was one of Ernie's biggest fans."

"You were? I'm in touch with his sister, Jan. She's the one who gave me the name of Dick Hardin."

"Ernie was one of my very good friends," Courtney said sadly. "He piloted several of my recoveries. The best way to describe him was a complete gentleman. A very handsome man with a great smile, and always cool under pressure.

"I carried him out of the wreckage. I knew it was

Ernie because when I got inside the aircraft, I recognized his maroon helmet. I tried not to look at him as I picked him up. I didn't feel anything when I carried him out and I've always felt bad about that."

"You had a job to do. It's perfectly understandable you had to 'shut down' in order to perform. What an awful feeling to carry out a friend."

"I'll tell you what I'm going to do. I have diaries and copies of statements on the crash. I'm going to write up a step-by-step account of what happened and send it to you."

"Oh, that would mean a lot to me! Thank you so much for doing all of this for me."

"My dear, I was extremely touched when I read what you sent to O.C. It was a very poignant letter and touched my heart. You have questions and they need answers. If I can answer any of them, it will be my pleasure. Now, you work in Beaverton, Oregon, don't you? Exactly where is that?"

"It's actually a suburb of Portland."

"Very good! My wife Donna and I are going to Japan in November. And by strange coincidence, we're stopping in Portland for two days on our way home."

"You're kidding!" I exclaimed. "Do you have family or friends here?"

"Well, Donna was a flight attendant for several years and flew into Portland. She always wanted to return for a visit and I've never been there. So we planned a little layover to go through your city. We would very much like to meet you and maybe go out to dinner while we're there, if you would like."

"Oh, Courtney, it would be my pleasure."

"Well, my dear. Then we will meet in November and I can't wait!" Courtney said. "I'll work on my account of that day and get it off to you in the next few days. Let me end this conversation by saying I don't believe there are any better men than corpsmen. Your father was extremely brave and definitely someone to look up to. The sole fact he volunteered to fly medevac missions shows just what a courageous man he really was."

My eyes filled with tears as Courtney said such kind things about my father. "Thank you, Courtney. That means more than you can ever know," I said quietly. As we started to say our good-byes, I remembered one more thing I needed to tell him.

"Courtney? Welcome home."

WITHIN JUST A FEW DAYS, I RECEIVED THE PACKAGE Courtney promised.

August 14, 1998

Dear Stephanie,

Several days ago I talked with Colonel Owen C. Baker USMC (Ret.), "O.C." as he is known, who was my immediate superior in Vietnam. We have been very close friends since those dark days and our friendship grows with the years. An honorable and sincere man, Colonel Baker wanted to share your story with me as I was involved in the events of that February day, primarily to extricate the crew of your father's aircraft and provide medical assistance to the survivors.

As stated, he was the Aircraft Maintenance Officer of HMM 364 and I was the Maintenance Control Officer. Additionally, I led a helicopter recovery team, which airlifted (or salvaged) helicopters which went down, or had problems while flying. Before I begin, please bear with me as I would like to take a moment to touch on HMM 364, the "Purple Foxes."

I joined the squadron just about the same time as your father arrived at MAG 11 during September 1968. HMM 364 will always have a place in my heart because of the wonderful unselfish men who were in the unit. Not exactly "saints," sometimes outrageous, they were always brave, dedicated men who did everything expected of them and more. I certainly include your father in that sentiment. All the Navy Corpsmen and Navy Doctors were treasured by the Marine units.

Our unit provided troop movement, logistic re-supply, and the very important medical evacuations. The Navy Corpsmen were normally attached to the base hospital, or in Marine terms "Sick Bay." This was the case with your father. Assigned to MAG 16 at Marble Mountain, he was one of the Corpsmen who volunteered to fly the MedEvac missions.

Our Squadron Flight Surgeon, Lt. Clay Linkous USN (Medical Corps), is another person I have close contact with. He went on most recoveries with my team and we have been close friends since Vietnam. He lives not too far from me in Florida. I talked with him last night, and asked about your father. As your father was a new guy, Dr. Linkous can't recall many personal details, however, he kept a daily journal, and he had your father's name and the other Corpsman's name as having been killed on 7 February. We talked of how deeply it affected him at the time and even now, after almost thirty years the pain is still with him. This pain haunts all of us, as Colonel Baker said, "your request has brought back very deeply felt and aching memories."

So, this preamble leads us in to the day of 7 February 1969. I will give you the facts as I know them. When we meet in Portland you may ask me all the questions you would like regarding the following information and I will do my best to answer them.

====================================

Completed 17 August, 1998

Stephanie,

The following narrative are my memories regarding the loss of HMM 364 CH-46D, call sign: "Swift 1-1." The facts I present here have been checked against documentation in my possession and from personal notes kept by me, memory and unit award write-ups.

The day of 7 February, 1969 found two CH-46D helicopters flying from the Marble Mountain Air Facility as medical evacuation aircraft. Their call signs were "Swift 1-1" and "Swift 1-2." Swift 1-1 was piloted by Captain Ernie Bartolina and Swift 1-2 piloted by Lt. Dick Hardin. (Captain Bartolina was the lead and Lt. Hardin the wingman.) They were to provide medical support for Marine Infantry operations near the village of An Hoa in what was called "Arizona Territory." This area had been a thorn in the side of our forces for some time. No matter how often we swept through the area it was never cleared of North Vietnamese military.

On this day the weather was cloudy, low overcast and intermittent rain. At some point, I believe to be early afternoon, the two helicopters were directed to a certain area (map coordinates AT820561) to pick up several badly wounded Marines. I am not certain of the unit they were attached to, however, I would guess it to be 3rd Battalion 26th Marines, 3rd Marine Division. I must assume the weather was deteriorating because Captain Bartolina was having a tough time getting into the zone to pick the wounded up. As Colonel Baker told you in his letter "people said he attempted to get to the Marines on the ground by having them talk to him on the radio and guide him based on the sound of his helicopter."

At some point during his approach the aircraft was hit with enough enemy fire to bring it down. The impact was hard, sudden, and mortal. There was no fire, it hit in a rice paddy with water about 10 inches deep. Fuel from the ruptured tanks covered everything. Lt. Hardin landed with two Air Force personnel. I am certain hostile fire was intense and these people had no time to get the crew from the aircraft as it was flattened and twisted. I believe they picked up one person, however, I heard later he expired before they could land (I cannot verify this). I have no idea where Lt. Hardin got the Air Force men. Their names were SSgt. Ramirez and Sgt. J.J. Cromer – both of the 366th Civil Engineers Squadron. I suspect they came from the base at An Hoa, which was just across a river from where they went down.

*As soon as it was known Swift 1-1 was down I was
informed and alerted our recovery team. Someone, I
can't remember who, said "take cutting tools" which
we did. Within minutes we were on our way to the
crash site in Swift 2-3, another CH-46D helicopter.*

*Our pilot was Lt. Thomas Sullivan and the co-pilot Lt.
William Beebe. Once on the scene we were told by a
gunship (call sign "Hostage Victor") that air strikes
were in progress, the zone extremely "hot" and to orbit
at a safe distance. While orbiting at two thousand feet
we received a hit in our left-hand fuel cell. After several
minutes we started our approach into the zone, both
gunners and the crew chief were shooting as we
touched down. Only then did I realize the infantry
Marines on the ground were still engaged and here we
were stopped cold as soon as we jumped out of the
helicopter. Several wounded were quickly put on the
helicopter as it was lifting off. Dr. Linkous helped load
the wounded and then joined me. I found myself with
all the other team members crouched behind
tombstones. We had gotten out on the edge of an old
French cemetery and the wreckage of your father's
aircraft was about eighty five yards away from us. We
could not move for a few minutes (one reason I did not
want to move was I wanted to make sure all of my team
was together and none had been hit). I told three of my
Sergeants to follow me and told the rest to stay in the
cemetery until we gave them the signal to follow. As we
ran across the rice paddy I noticed Dr. Linkous was
also with me. We had some air cover (Marine A-4 Sky
Hawks) but they soon departed because they were low
on fuel. When they departed things got much hotter.
The North Vietnamese knew when to keep their heads*

down and when not to (air cover made the job much easier). The four of us ran to the wrecked CH-46D.

At this point Stephanie, let me say the men in the wreckage could have been asleep. They died on impact, none of them suffered. Using cutting tools and our hands we removed the bodies from the fuselage and Dr. Linkous checked each of them as we did this. I carried Ernie Bartolina myself not feeling anything even though I was one of his biggest fans. In retrospect, I was numb and in a hurry. All our efforts were done as quickly as humanly possible because there was a tremendous amount of fuel lying on top of the water and inside the aircraft. We put the bodies up against a rice paddy dike thirty or forty meters away and I assembled the rest of my team with the exception of Cpl. (later Sgt.) Kiselewsky who was still in the cemetery covering our activity by firing his machine gun into a bamboo tree line to the north of us. During this, we stopped several times to lay in the water because the bad guys were still shooting at us and we were in the open with absolutely no cover. Then, thank God, we got more air cover.

Several Air Force airplanes (A-1 SkyRaiders) arrived and started to really work over two bamboo tree lines – one to the north and another southwest of us where the North Vietnamese, I'm sure, had heavy caliber guns. I am certain the guys who shot your father down were probably the same people shooting at us. The Air Force aircraft turned the bamboo tree lines into bamboo splinters. They gave us outstanding support. As I think back, I would guess the people manning the North Vietnamese guns also had a very bad day. During this time it started to rain again and darkness rapidly approached. Two of my team and myself returned to the aircraft one last time to make sure we removed everyone and everything.

Lt. Sullivan and Lt. Beebe returned to the medical station to deliver the wounded Marines and landed at the Marble Mountain Air Facility to inspect the battle damage to their aircraft (which was not enough to stop them from returning to the Arizona Territory). I radioed for an "extract" simply meaning we were ready to be picked up. It was 1915 (7:15 PM) when I made the call. Lt. Sullivan made a high speed, low level approach to a spot just yards from us. We loaded everything and everyone on board including three machine guns from the downed aircraft. We worked very quickly, but there was no panic, no rushing. Then Lt. Sullivan took off and as we lifted out it was dark enough then to see the North Vietnamese firing at us, and we returned fire until we were out of their range. A helicopter lifting into the air before it can get its speed up, or, when it has slowed down to land such as Captain Bartolina tried to do, makes an ideal target. This was the life and the fear of all helicopter crews in Vietnam. Knowing this, I never cease to admire those brave men, pilots, crew chiefs, gunners, Corpsmen – like Gary N. Young and the thousands like him who were so unselfish and took off each day trying to save other young Americans.

There is no epilogue here Stephanie, but for you I hope there is closure. We will meet in Portland, and I will get to meet a Naval Hero's daughter. I think we will have a good visit and as I said; I will answer any questions you have to the best of my ability. If you do

166

not mind I will send a copy of this to Colonel Baker,
Dr. Linkous and my longtime friend, Sgt. Richard
Kiselewsky, the machine gunner that covered our work
from the cemetery. He is now a retired policeman and
has a farm in New Jersey – another hero who continues
to be one of my best friends. Each of these gentlemen
knows of your quest to get to know you father and the
circumstances surrounding his death. Again, I refer to
Colonel Baker's letter: "with a caring daughter like you
it is obvious he was a caring man himself and his
character and legacy lives in you."

By the way, I thank you for the "welcome home." May I
also say; God bless you Stephanie. You too are a hero.

The tears flowed as I finished reading this report. If not for the heroics of these brave men, my father could very well have been forever listed as MIA. But the men on this team proved unquestionably Marines take care of their own. It wasn't just a statement, but the way they lived their lives.

COURTNEY AND I CONTINUED TO CORRESPOND with dozens of emails and many phone calls until finally, he and Donna arrived in Portland. Fittingly, I met these two wonderful people on November 3rd, which would have been Gary's 50th birthday.

After work, it poured rain as it can only in Portland, so I picked them up in front of their hotel, instead of trying to find a parking spot. When I drove up in my little Metro, I saw them standing in the doorway, huddled under an umbrella. First, Donna dodged through the raindrops and jumped in the back seat of my car. Even in the tight quarters of my tiny car, we managed a great big hug. Courtney hopped in next and as we hugged, I marveled that the man who risked his life to recover my father's body sat next to me. From the moment we met, the three of us felt comfortable, as if we had always known each other. As Courtney stated many times during the last couple of months, we were family now.

Over dinner, we didn't talk about the helicopter crash, but we did discuss Vietnam. Courtney had story after story about HMM-364 and was more than happy to share them. He went to Vietnam for three tours, the first one accomplished on a civilian passport in the early stages of planning the war. His third tour was with the Foxes and he further helped me understand the mystique behind the unit.

"In the late summer of 1968, the unit was in a state of transition," Courtney began. "Personnel changed very quickly and we had a rough time. But in early 1969, Gene Brady entered as the new Commanding Officer." Pride and love entered into his voice. "He was a former enlisted man, a former fighter pilot, and had a truck load of common sense, personal excellence and a fantastic sense of humor. He was an outstanding Marine with a deep respect for his men and the job they were doing. No one realized at the time the profound impact this man would have on the unit and the individual lives of his men. No one will ever know, but it was, and is, strongly suspected Gene Brady was hand-picked to get this squadron up and going. It was common-place for him to be in the maintenance shack at 0130, talking to a crew chief on the flight line at 0200, and then flying an early resupply or medevac the next morning.

"We had a lot of losses during this time period, your

father's incident being one of them. When we lost a crew or an individual, we grieved, usually by drinking into the night talking about the lost crew and what happened to them, but the next day, returned to business as usual. Of course it was hard to lose a friend and squadron mate, but no one dwelled on it. The squadron closed ranks tighter; the adversity of the loss was the cement which bound the squadron ever closer.

"During this tough time, Gene could be found anywhere and everywhere. He had a special relationship with the crew chiefs and gunners. He would make sure his jeep was available every night so maintenance could go steal whatever was needed!"

We all laughed at this. Fascinated by Courtney's stories, I didn't interrupt with questions or comments and just let him talk.

"Gene was the perfect Commanding Officer for this unit at this critical time. Never heavy-handed, he led by example. When a crew was lost, he hurt as much as any other member of the unit. He was much loved then, as he is much loved today thirty years later.

"He had a pet goose who would crap on anyone he was handed to," Courtney chuckled. "Gene delighted in letting wing headquarters people, and others considered 'useless,' hold his goose!

"Purple Fox behavior became legendary. 'Screw You Grunt' was jokingly marked on the bottom of one CH-46 with white chalk, while dropping a resupply of not just the usual C-rats and water, but also candy bars, cokes and lots of girlie magazines. This kindness prompted an Assistant Division Commander to come in one afternoon in a Huey, look up Gene Brady and thank the Purple Foxes on behalf of his division.

"Our gunners loved sticking flowers in the muzzle of

their .50 cal guns. We also caught them inserting hand grenades into small jars, like baby food jars, so when they took fire they could toss out their nasty little bombs.

"Members of other squadrons liked to sit with the Purple Foxes at the club simply because it was fun and something unexpected always seemed to happen. Colonel Brady was always in hot water because of the conduct of his officers. But he always stood up for them and enjoyed a loyalty and a following bordering on worship. He would deny this, but, during that spring, it was a fact."

Courtney told us story after story giving me his invaluable insight into the unit. I won't ever forget his stories, especially those of Gene Brady, our beloved Papa Fox.

After dinner, we drove back to their hotel. They invited me up to their room to continue our visit, and I brought along all the information I gathered in my search. One item was a map I recently received from another veteran. It showed the locations of DaNang, Marble Mountain and the Arizona Territory in Vietnam. The area where Gary's helicopter crashed had been marked from the coordinates Courtney previously gave me.

"Did I get this right? Is this the location of my father's crash?" I asked.

Courtney examined the map closely and replied, "That's exactly right. I'll never forget it."

He and Donna looked through my three-ring binder in which I attempted to keep straight all the material I accumulated.

One page held the eleven black and white photographs Gary took in Vietnam.

I excitedly pulled them out. "I've been waiting forever to have someone tell me about these pictures."

Courtney took the tiny stack of pictures from me and flipped through them. "Flight tower, two-holer, one-holer, four-holer, what was probably his hootch, another two-holer, a local village ... "

I stared at Courtney in amazement. I knew what he was talking about. "You mean of the eleven pictures my father took, almost all of them are of toilets?" I exclaimed.

Courtney burst out laughing. "Well, sweetheart, they were very important to us!"

"Men!"

Finally, after midnight, Courtney escorted me to my car. As we rode down in the elevator, I needed to ask one more question.

"Courtney, what was really the true condition of the helicopter?"

"It was a very smashed up aircraft. It looked to me as if it crashed almost upright, but then turned over on its side as the force from the crash propelled it forward. Absolutely flattened like someone stomped on a tin can. It crashed into a rice paddy and we were scratched and cut up because of the wreckage, as well as burning and stinging from the raw jet fuel, which we waded around in.

"The men were very banged up and bruised, but miraculously, not as bad as it would appear from the condition of the helicopter. I do know they didn't suffer, Stephanie. The impact was just too sudden and forceful."

That question had lurked in the back of my mind, and once I heard the answer, I felt relieved. On top of everything else, Courtney gave me a measure of peace.

ELEVEN

HEARING WHAT HAPPENED ON THE DAY MY
father died from all the different viewpoints put the
pieces of a puzzle together. From men who flew other
missions that day, to those listening back at base in the
ready room, to Courtney's description of the recovery,
each perspective helped complete the overall picture.

One such piece of the puzzle came in a letter from
Ernest Cunningham, a retired Colonel. A pilot with the
Purple Foxes, he flew the day my father died, earning
one of the three Distinguished Flying Crosses he
received during his time in Vietnam.

Dear Stephanie,

*I was the Operations Officer of HMM-364 during the
period of your father's death in Vietnam and do have
some personal knowledge of the people involved and the
accident. I am enclosing a handout from the memorial
service and as you can see there were six people lost in
this flight.*

*The pilot, Ernie Bartolina was a very quiet, handsome
and capable Marine. I had been with Ernie since July,*

1968 when I joined the squadron at Phu Bai. He was my assistant in the Administrative Department before I moved to Operations.

The accident occurred in the afternoon because I remember talking to Ernie just before I launched on an afternoon mission. He and his crew were still on the ground at Marble Mountain on MEDIVAC standby when I launched. I was flying with the Squadron Commander, Lt. Col. Eugene R. Brady. Some time into our mission we were diverted to the crash scene by DaNang Direct Air Support Center, DASC, to assist in the recovery effort.

However, shortly after arriving over the site in the Arizona Area, we were again diverted to an emergency recovery of a reconnaissance team. I objected to this diversion, since it was our aircraft involved, but was assured the recovery of our aircraft was underway and was told to comply with my new mission.

That was the extent of my first-hand involvement but after returning to Marble Mountain later that afternoon I was briefed on the loss of the crew and the incident involved. As I remember, the aircraft was hit by ground fire during an emergency MEDIVAC pick up and went out of control, impacting the ground in such a way that all were lost immediately on impact.

First Lieutenant Moke was relatively new to the Squadron and I remember him only during our meetings in the ready room and a couple of times he flew as my co-pilot. The other two Marines aboard, Charles Miller and Rodney Shank, were the crew chief and the gunner. I am sorry to say I don't remember Gary as he was new to MEDIVAC and I believe being checked out by Hospitalman Second Class Walter Ripley Tyrrell during this specific flight. I knew First Lieutenant Richard Hardin but have been unable to get his present address for you. I will continue to try for this information and forward it when I do.

The fact that Gary was a Corpsman does allow me to provide a bit of insight on Gary and as to his motivation for volunteering for the MEDIVAC mission. Corpsmen are highly respected by Marines, and especially by Marines like me who flew MEDIVAC missions in combat. Navy Corpsmen are a cut above the rest of us. To be a Corpsman in the Navy a standard of maturity, intelligence, motivation and compassion exists which exceeds the average Sailor or Marine.

Whether they serve on the ground with the infantry or in the air on MEDIVAC missions, Corpsmen always seem to be there when you need them.

I can honestly say I never met a Corpsman I did not like and respect. I know I liked and respected Gary even though I have no specific memory of him. He volunteered because he met these high standards.

I am sorry I cannot provide you with any additional information. If there is anything I can do for you in the future please contact me.

Sincerely, Ernest C. Cunningham
Colonel USMC (Retired)

Along with his letter came a copy of the memorial service program, the same program from the box of Gary's things.

This one simple act underlined the selflessness of these men. To have saved this program for over thirty years meant he must have treasured it dearly, as he treasured his friendship with Ernie Bartolina. And yet, the moment he received my letter, he instantly sent it to me.

Even though I had a copy of the program already, something made me hesitate in returning it. And several months later, I discovered why. One of the sisters of the men who died with my father had never seen one, and I gave it to her, knowing she would treasure it as I did mine.

AT THIS POINT, I HAD SEARCHED FOR DICK HARDIN for over a year, hoping his viewpoint from the chase helicopter would round out the details of the crash. There were other men from the crew aboard this bird, but with no names how could I figure out which Purple Foxes were on board? I had to wait for them to find me.

To: Stephanie Hanson
From: Jim Bandish
Date: Mon, Aug 03, 1998 1:17pm

Late on the afternoon of 7 February 1969 I was flying as a crew chief on the second of two medevac choppers. The lead chopper was shot down and crashed in Quang Nam Province. While the picture looks familiar, I cannot say I remember the Corpsman. We would have various corpsmen fly with us on medevac missions. As you may know this type of duty was on volunteer basis and very dangerous. I was told that out of our original

*32 aircraft, 12 were shot down. Every corpsman I flew
with was a hero by just performing their duties aboard
a chopper and I never saw any perform in any fashion
contrary to this belief. I do not know if this was the
same crash, however I do remember this one quite well
as I saw the lead chopper go in. There was no fire, but a
tremendous impact. No one should have suffered in this
crash. I may have some paperwork in the attic with
names of some of the other people who were in this
squadron. I heard someone did survive the crash but it
was never confirmed, a gunner I think. The crew
usually consisted of a pilot, co-pilot, corpsman, two
gunners and a crew chief on medevac missions. Good
Luck.*

*Sincerely,
Jim Bandish*

This *had* to be my father's crash, which meant Jim
flew as the crew chief on Dick Hardin's helicopter. I
quickly sent Jim a reply with all my information, hoping
to help clarify which crash he saw.

A couple of weeks went by with no reply, but I
wasn't willing to lose this lead. I sent Jim another quick
email, in case he hadn't received my original reply, and
this time he emailed back.

To:	**Stephanie Hanson**
From:	**Jim Bandish**
Date:	**Fri, Aug 21, 1998 5:55pm**

*Based on the date, location and no other crash on land
that day, I believe it was the same crash. If you would
like to know what happened that day I can provide you*

with some information as the chopper I was in became involved in the recovery work. I believe there were several ground marines killed related to this recovery, as I extracted several wounded ground marines.

Nine more may have died as it turned into a considerable fire fight. This landing was supposed to be a piece of cake. I will probably remember that crash for the rest of my life. No one else in my plane saw the crash happen or knew exactly where the plane went in. It was a very chilling experience and seemed to last forever.

The mission consisted of two CH-46 Sea Knight Helicopters. One chopper would go into the zone, while the other circled overhead in case of a problem. Usually the choppers took turns going into a zone, however, not with medevac missions. Normally only one chopper, of the two, carried a corpsman. So this chopper would always go into the zone if the injury to ground personnel was very serious. This was the case that day. Also, there was a procedure to enter a zone. The pilot would be in contact with the ground forces and ask certain questions.

1. When was the last time you received any fire or enemy contact at your position? The answer that day: none from that position.

2. If you would receive any fire, from which direction would you likely receive it? Answer: not likely to receive from any direction.

The pilot would then have the ground forces pop a

smoke at their location. The color of the smoke would not be mentioned to avoid having the bad guys popping a smoke of the same color. Next, the pilot would confirm a smoke on the ground when he saw it – i.e. I have a yellow smoke at my three o'clock. Next, the ground personnel would confirm the pilot's statement – i.e. That's a 10-4. We have you at our nine o'clock. Next, the pilot would decide on the best way to enter the zone taking into consideration such things as trees, clearance, zone configuration, wind, etc. However the most important consideration was where the bad guys were. No one thought there were any bad guys there that day, but there were many of them there. I think most of them were in a nearby FRIENDLY village and just to the right of the village.

Anyway there was a little light cloud cover that day, probably at three thousand feet, below it was clear to the ground. The lead chopper started its approach into the zone and we lost visual contact with it in the clouds. Usually the two choppers fly in a circular pattern when entering a zone and across from one another, so one can watch the other. This was the case that day. I looked out the crew chief's window when the other chopper broke through the clouds toward the zone. Suddenly the chopper did a nose up flip and rotated a full 360 degrees and went in wheels first into a rice paddy. It actually looked like an aerobatic maneuver and a landing. I thought the light or angle may have created an illusion and the chopper did make a safe landing, it really appeared that way. Suddenly I heard the pilot or co-pilot say, "Oh my God, the plane went in. Did anyone see where it went in?" I answered "yes" and told the pilot it was off to his 230 about a

*quarter of a mile from us. There was no further radio
contact with the downed plane.*

*Anyway I kept telling the pilot to turn until we were
lined up with the downed plane. The pilot made visual
contact and we proceeded to land where the downed
chopper was located. We were within approximately
100 feet of the downed bird when all hell broke loose.
We started receiving intense fire from our six o'clock
(rear) and we could not return fire to this location
because of it being behind us. The pilot then proceeded
out of the area. A second attempt was made to get into
the area. This time the gunners sprayed the area. Once
again we got within approximately 100 feet of the
downed plane and received intense enemy fire and
could not land.*

*Additional fire support was called for, also the ground
forces moved into the area to secure the area near the
downed chopper, while we went back to pick up a crew
with extraction tools to open up the downed chopper.
Next we went back to the downed chopper. By now the
fixed-wing aircraft were there laying down cover fire
and also dropping smoke canisters between the bad
guys and the downed chopper. This permitted choppers
to enter the zone, while the fire was still heavy, the bad
guys could not see you. I dropped off the extraction
team and picked up a wounded marine. This process
continued until the crew was extracted. The downed
chopper was burned in place after recovering the crew.*

*I heard one person survived, but found it very difficult
to believe. If so, I can understand why he does not care
to relive that day. This is about as much as I can*

remember about that day. It's been almost thirty years
and I cannot remember ever telling this story but I
remember it very well.

While in Viet Nam I flew 504 combat missions. Out of
all of this, this was the only time I saw anyone die. We
had a lot of people killed in my squadron, but I never
saw it occur. The strange thing about it was in many
cases it was a strange twist of fate. The first time,
someone filling in for someone else or doing something
extra. I had three friends from my hooch killed like that,
two on their first mission, one filling in for another guy
who got sick. McDaniels only had two weeks left on his
tour and did not have to do any more flying. By
volunteering, he died 30 minutes later. You just can't
figure it out.

There was other activity in the area related to ground
forces and other aircraft of which I am not aware from
which you may be able to gather additional info. Well, I
have said enough, probably too much. Telling this story
has made me feel very sad, but yet very happy in
sharing it with you. It is a very strange feeling. I hope
this helps you with closure. Just remember your father
and Jan's brother did a much needed job and they did
not have to do it. Many, many lives were saved with
helicopters; the death toll in Viet Nam would have been
ten-fold if not for corpsmen and medevac crews. All
were heroes doing heroic actions every day.

I have attached a few pictures, I will send more. If you
wouldn't mind, would you send this to Jan too? I don't
think I can write it again. Please excuse the grammar. I
think I'll go sit down and have a good cigar. I am very

sorry for the loss of your father and Jan's brother, we did everything we could.

Sincerely,
Jim Bandish

Almost thirty years went by without Jim ever talking about this incident, yet he could recall this day with absolute clarity. Many of us can't remember details from recent events. With all of these accounts, my picture was nearly complete.

TWELVE

EVEN THOUGH I UNRAVELED THE MAJORITY OF the mysteries surrounding my father's death, I knew I would never be satisfied until I knew the truth about whether or not a survivor existed. But even after receiving over one hundred emails, no one could confirm a survivor.

And then, Rich Kiselewsky came forward with the one piece of information I so desperately wanted to learn.

To:	*Stephanie Hanson*
From:	*Rich Kiselewsky*
Date:	*Sun, Aug 16, 1998 8:04am*

Dear Stephanie:

I'm responding to your inquiry, which I found in PUSHTruck Mailing, a newsletter for Helicopter Marines.

I am also aware of your inquiry through former Marine Major Courtney Payne, with whom you have communicated and with whom I still keep in touch.

*I was a member of the recovery team inserted into the
crash zone and assisted in the recovery of all those KIA
on the aircraft, including your dad. While not
extremely familiar with him, I did meet him on a
number of occasions and have a general recollection of
his appearance.*

*I can recall his dedication and heroics and esprit de
corps, providing valuable support to our comrades who
were wounded in action and medevaced.*

*You mentioned a lone survivor in the aircraft. That is
in fact correct. His name is Greg Tomaro, and although
I have his address, there is no phone number given. I
and others have attempted to communicate with him, to
no avail. Perhaps he will respond to your inquiry.*

Respectfully,
Rich Kiselewsky

And there it was. The survivor's name, just like that.
One person. Someone who knew exactly what my father
went through in the last moments of his life. This
extraordinary thought almost frightened me. But what if
he didn't want to talk to me? If he didn't want to talk to
his friends from Vietnam, why would I be any different?

That evening I called Rich. Rich stands six feet five
inches, weighs over 230 pounds and is a retired New
York Port Authority cop. And his voice matched it,
strong, deep and with a prominent New York accent.

"Stephanie!" he exclaimed enthusiastically. "I'm so
glad you called."

"Oh, I had to Rich," I replied. "There was no way I
could express my thanks by email. I wanted to let you

know although I've already received over one hundred emails and asked time and time again if anyone remembered a survivor, every single person said no. And then I got your email today. You are the *only one* who knew of a survivor. I was beginning to give up hope."

"Oh, Greg was very badly injured though and I'm not surprised many people thought he died also. But I'm surprised I'm the only one who remembered his name. He was a good friend to several of us."

"So, how much effort has been made to contact him?" I asked cautiously.

"Well, several of us tried to send him mail over the years," Rich answered. "We never could get a phone number nor answers to any of the letters. The address I have is rather old, but maybe you can start with that."

"I will definitely try. It's a good start. Rich, I can't thank you enough for sending me your email. And I can't believe you remember my father. I know most of the Marines didn't really know the corpsmen."

"I remember your dad from when he transferred down to Marble Mountain. I ran the armory and assigned him his weapon. Like I said, I don't recall much, but his face is definitely familiar to me. I knew it was your dad out there on the recovery mission."

"Yes, Courtney sent me a write-up. Thank you so much for what you did. I know what a harrowing rescue it was and I'll be forever grateful to all of you."

"Courtney told me he has sent a little package to you in an effort to bring all you have learned together. I hope it helps if even just a little," Rich said. "Courtney was one of the bravest Marines I have ever met. He's a little guy, hell, most all are when you're as big as I am, with a very large heart. As a result of our time together in

Vietnam we've become very good friends."

"I don't even know if I can find the words to explain how much talking to you and Courtney means to me."

Rich quietly listened as I filled him in on the details of my adoption and my search.

"Your dad is probably looking down on you right now with a great big proud smile on his face, seeing how well his little girl has grown into the young woman you are today. Indeed, he left you in his place and you do him honor," Rich said gruffly.

I couldn't help being struck again at how warm and loving these men could be. It felt like my father left a whole group of men here on earth to take care of me.

THE NEXT DAY I THOUGHT ABOUT HOW TO contact Greg Tomaro. I first went on the internet and tried to find a phone number for him in the city he lived, but couldn't find anything.

So that night I sat down and composed the most difficult letter I ever wrote. How do you write and ask someone if they were the lone survivor of a crash without bringing back horrific memories? I tried to make it as non-intrusive as possible, but I doubt I succeeded.

The next morning I dropped the letter in the mail, thinking how great the odds must be that I would never hear from him.

One week later, my phone rang at work and I heard a female voice. "Stephanie, my name is Jane Tomaro. I'm Greg Tomaro's ex-wife. I received the letter you wrote to Greg. But we've actually been divorced for over ten years. I opened your letter not even noticing who it was addressed to. I'm so sorry. Do you think you could send him a new letter? I can give you his address."

I was so taken aback I didn't know what to say, but finally managed to speak and hoped I appeared calmer than I felt. "Of course, no problem. Go ahead and give me the address."

She rattled off the address and we said good-bye. I immediately printed up a duplicate letter and mailed it off to the new address.

It's unsettling to realize just how close I came to never making contact with Greg. If his ex-wife *had* thrown the letter away or not called me, I don't think I ever would have attempted to contact Greg again. I would have assumed he received the letter and didn't want to respond and would have respected his decision.

As the next few weeks passed with no reply, I wondered if my lucky streak had come to an end. And then the phone rang.

"Stephanie? This is Greg Tomaro," the caller said.

Before I could collect my thoughts and answer, he asked, "I'm wondering, how did you find me?"

He didn't sound mad, but not quite happy either. "I got your name and old address from Rich Kiselewsky," I said cautiously. "Your ex-wife received my first letter and called me with your current address."

He paused for a few moments, and when he spoke again, it wasn't quite as gruff. "Your letter was very disconcerting to receive. I wasn't going to respond to it at first. In fact, I was going to just throw it away. Then I started feeling I owed it to you to call. But, I'm not sure I can be of much help."

"I really don't have any specific questions. I just had a need inside of me to get in touch with you. I'm not really sure of the reason. I just felt it was important to speak with you."

"I'll tell you right off I really don't recall much about

the accident," Greg said quietly.

At this moment, I should have been extremely disappointed. But, the instant the words were out of his mouth, I realized just making contact with Greg was the important thing. I searched for him for months, wanting to ask all sorts of questions, but now it didn't matter. Somehow, just talking to Greg connected me with my father in a way I couldn't explain.

"It's all right," I said. "In fact, I have learned quite a lot about the accident since I wrote you." I tried to describe my communications with Courtney Payne, Rich Kiselewsky, Jim Bandish, but it was difficult for me to talk about the accident with him. I knew it had to bring up all sorts of memories and feelings I couldn't even fathom.

"Like I said, I don't remember much," Greg said. "I remember we tried to land in a really bad place. It surprised us. We had no warning of any hostile fire in the area before we went in. The last thing I remember is the helicopter flipping over and then I lost consciousness. I don't really remember anything after that.

"As a matter of fact, one of the reasons I called was because you mentioned Ernie Bartolina's name in your letter."

"I'm in touch with Ernie's sister, Jan," I replied. "She found me several months ago and we've been searching for answers together."

"I can't believe you're in touch with Ernie's family," Greg said. "Will you please pass a message along to her for me?"

"Of course I will. I talk to her often."

"Tell her I credit Ernie for saving my life. Even after we were hit, Ernie stayed calm and relayed information over the radio and headset to us so everyone knew what was going on. Due to Ernie there was no panic. He was a true hero."

He had difficulty speaking and I choked up too. "I'm sorry for asking you to bring up such memories," I apologized.

He adamantly responded, "You don't owe me any apologies, Stephanie. I'm just sorry I can't help you any more than this."

"You've already helped me more than you can realize," I replied.

"I can at least tell you about Vietnam. This accident happened on my second tour. I first arrived in Vietnam in January of 1968 and basically flew the whole time. It meant a lot to me to be doing something productive over there, as most of the war seemed so bureaucratical. I felt like I accomplished something by being direct support for the infantry. Many of our medevac flights went out without a corpsman on board. The medevac flights were some of the most dangerous, but for some reason whenever we had a corpsman on board, I always felt so much safer. I knew they would know what to do in order to help save the lives of the men we picked up. In fact, I had so much respect for the corpsmen that later on in the States I became an EMT."

"Yes, I'm finding out just how special the Marines think of their corpsmen."

"I left Vietnam in November of 1968 but decided to extend for another six months. I arrived back in Vietnam in the beginning of February of 1969 and I believe we crashed on my first mission since arriving back in-country."

"I'll bet that's why it took me so long to find out your name," I said. "Have you talked with any of those guys?"

"No. And I really don't know why. There's no good

reason for it. In fact, I'm always hearing of my uncles going off to World War II or Korean reunions and often ask myself why I don't have the same urge to connect with any of the guys from Vietnam. I don't have an answer; I just never got the urge to do so."

"I think it's something you can't force," I said. "But maybe someday you will want to. If you ever do, just let me know and I can put you in touch with some of them. And I'm sure the Pop A Smoke organization would be able to help you out even more."

"What's Pop A Smoke?" he asked.

"It's the United States Marine Corps Vietnam Helicopter Association. Pop A Smoke is their nickname. Anyone who served on helicopters in Vietnam can join. Actually they just let me join in lieu of my father, so I'm an FNG."

Greg laughed. "It's been a while since I've heard that term."

"They've been wonderful to me. I've been in touch with so many veterans since I found them and have learned so much about Vietnam from all of them. One of the things I've heard a lot about lately is survivor's guilt," I said. "That's one of the reasons I feel so bad about digging into your past."

"I actually don't feel too much survivor's guilt. I know God picked me to survive for a reason. I just don't know what it is. I recently turned fifty and I started thinking maybe I haven't really accomplished anything yet. In that way, I feel like I've let the other six guys down."

"Greg, if the only reason you were chosen to survive was to talk to me, then that's enough," I said sincerely. "And I do feel it is one of the reasons. Somehow, someone knew I would need to speak to you. And want to tell you there is someone here who thinks of you guys as heroes and I want to welcome you home, even if it is thirty years late."

We both cried openly now. "I'm glad I called you, Stephanie. This wasn't as bad as I thought it and it has helped me."

"And vice versa, Greg. I will never be able to thank you enough."

"I hope you have a good life, Stephanie. Good-bye."

"And I wish the same to you, Greg. Good-bye."

As I hung up the phone, I assumed this was our one and only conversation. He hadn't given me his phone number or any indication he wanted to talk again, and I would respect his wishes. This one phone call was precious enough to me.

OVER THE NEXT FEW DAYS, I WROTE AND TOLD my veteran friends of this latest development. To my surprise, lots of people did know Greg in Vietnam, but just hadn't realized he flew with my father. Many of them asked for his information to get in touch with him too. I didn't know how to handle these requests, since Greg and I talked about his reluctance to connect with any of his old friends. But I felt by not saying anything to Greg took the choice away from him. Maybe he didn't realize just how many people wanted to connect with him.

In the end, I wrote Greg another letter, telling him about all the requests. I promised not to bother him again if he didn't reply.

And, once again, a few weeks later, my phone rang.

"Stephanie, it's Greg Tomaro."

"I'm so sorry for bugging you again," I apologized.

"Oh, I'm beginning to get used to it," Greg laughed.

"I've thought a lot since your second letter. And I've decided I would like to hear from some of my old friends."

"I think that's fantastic. How do you want to do this? What is the best way for these guys to get in touch with you?"

Greg hesitated.

"How about if I find out their phone numbers and send them to you in a letter?" I asked. "That way you can contact them when you feel like it."

"Sounds like a good plan. I'm on the phone all day for work and don't typically answer my phone at home."

We talked for a little while longer and although not quite as apprehensive this time, he still didn't mention us keeping in touch in the future. Content to just act as the conduit, I thought it was great progress Greg changed his mind.

THAT EVENING, I RECEIVED A PHONE CALL FROM Bob "Steiny" Steinberg in response to my query letter.

"I was with HMM-364," Bob started out, "but out of country at the time of Gary's crash. I extended my tour in Vietnam for six months and in doing so I received a thirty-day leave. When I got back to HMM-364 on February 14th, I heard about the accident. What a horrible day. I knew many of the men involved in it all."

We threw some names back and forth and I mentioned talking to Greg earlier in the day.

"I've tried to get in touch with Greg for almost thirty years!" he exclaimed. "I was an extremely good friend of Greg's in Vietnam. In fact, when I returned to the States, Bill Barbier, another guy on your dad's recovery team, and I located him at MCAS Cherry Point and went to visit him, probably about November of 1969.

"I do remember hearing the first wave of Marines who found Greg presumed him to be dead. Greg could hear but couldn't move or speak. Then a corpsman came over and pronounced Greg still alive and called in a priority medevac. After Bill and I left, we discussed how good Greg looked, but how ill-at-ease and distracted he seemed. Given what he'd been through, we knew while physically okay, psychologically he would face years of recovery."

No wonder Greg would rather forget about that day.

Bob told me a few other stories about his time in Vietnam. One of them made a lasting impression on me.

"The men with the hardest time coming back from Vietnam were those who did things that could not be changed," Bob said. "One incident happened to me I still think about to this day.

"For three days we had unsuccessfully attempted to medevac badly wounded Marines from a mountainside near Hai Van Pass, just north of DaNang. I flew as the tail machine-gunner. We finally landed successfully and picked up seventeen wounded. Almost immediately after departing the landing zone, our aircraft crashed on the steep mountain-side, out-of-sight of the zone we just left.

"The crew chief told me to stand at the open door in the back of the aircraft and to shoot anything that moved in the tall elephant grass surrounding us. We knew we landed in an area with enemy troops and expected heavy fire. Soon, I saw movement and knew men headed towards us, but for some reason I waited until I could make a positive identification. Seconds later a man broke free from the grass and I recognized him as a

Marine and part of a rescue squad dispatched from the Marine's perimeter. The grunts heard us crash and came to help. I could have easily shot them. Our own troops. If I had, I don't know how I could have lived with it all of these years. Unfortunately, many men over there made mistakes such as this."

Over the years, Bob patiently answered all my questions and gave insight into the various aspects of a Vietnam veteran's life, as well as all those who serve our country. One of his most valuable contributions helped me understand the value of the words *welcome home*. Six years later, in writing to an Iraq veteran's mother who sought guidance on how to treat her returning son, he stated the following.

> *Communication is the key; that doesn't mean a streaming dialog. Sometimes a gesture, or a couple of words, can communicate more feeling than a half-hour speech. And a seemingly minor act could have a major positive effect on your Marine. I've learned that one of the most emotionally significant phrases heard by our Vietnam-era Foxes was something said by Stephanie Hanson at the end of her initial communication with them: "Welcome home." That simple phrase brought tears to many Marines' eyes more than thirty years after coming home. It was simple, sincere, supportive and appropriate. A mere two-word statement, but it communicated volumes.*

IN DECEMBER, I DECIDED TO SEND A CHRISTMAS card to Greg Tomaro, just to let him know I thought of him often. I dropped it in the outgoing mail slot at work and then retrieved my incoming mail. I laughed out loud to see a card from Greg sitting on the top of the stack! The note Greg wrote inside surprised me even more.

Stephanie,

I hope your holiday season is festive and joyous.

I may be going for some training at a plant near Seattle, WA. If that is close by, let me know. It will probably be late spring or summer. I'd like to meet you in person if that's ok with you.

Thank you and Semper Fi,
Greg

Seattle is less than three hours away from Portland, but I would have gone any distance to meet Greg face-to-face. However, with the proposed meeting still several months away, I constantly worried Greg would change his mind.

It was a joyous day when he called to confirm he would be in Seattle.

"I wondered if you still wanted to meet?" Greg asked.

"Absolutely! Just tell me when and where and I'll be there."

I scrambled for a pen and paper as he rattled off the dates and hotel location.

"Do you mind if I bring my brother along?" I asked. "He's a Marine too and I think you would have a lot to talk about."

"Sure," Greg said. "That way you won't have to drive by yourself."

I hoped bringing Geoff along would help keep the conversation flowing, and not always focused on the crash. Truthfully, I didn't know if Greg would even talk about it and I swore I wouldn't bring it up first.

The next Saturday morning Geoff and I headed to Seattle. On the drive up we ran into freeway construction which caused traffic to back-up for miles. The later it got, the more anxious I became. Already nervous to meet Greg, being late for our meeting really put me on edge.

Finally we arrived at the hotel. As we walked towards the entrance, I saw a very handsome, tall and slender man outside leaning up against a pillar and knew.

I walked up to him. "Greg?"

"Yes, Stephanie?"

I wanted to throw my arms around him in a big hug, but instead extended my hand out to shake. He had a good-natured air about him, although a slight amount of reserve in his greeting.

We drove down to Pike Street Market and after parking the car, we just walked around.

"You have no idea what changes have occurred in my life since I received your initial letter," Greg said.

"Um, is that good or bad?" I asked hesitantly.

"Oh, it's very good. I realized although I thought I put this all in the past, I really hadn't. You made me think of issues I needed to deal with. And thanks to you I contacted some of the guys and really enjoyed talking to them."

"Oh, I'm glad. I agonized over bothering you so many times, but it just felt like I had to do it."

"I even joined your Pop A Smoke organization," he said in a matter-of-fact tone and changed the subject.

As the day turned cold and misty, we headed up to the Space Needle. Greg and Geoff talked about being Marines and overseas experiences and I listened as they compared stories. Eventually we reached a restaurant and went inside.

"About the crash," Greg said quietly. "That day I was truly scared to death. When we received the fatal hits, Ernie knew we were going down. He kept relaying what was happening over our headsets and managed to keep everyone calm.

"I remember grabbing Miller to keep him from falling out the open door as the helicopter started to roll over. It's at this point my memory gets hazy. I remember being on the ground not being able to move or talk, but I could hear the ground units come up to me. One of the Marines pulled a large chunk of metal off of me and called for a corpsman."

"You said you knew Ernie fairly well. Did you know any of the other men?" I asked.

"Not that well, I knew Ernie the best. I remember the co-pilot was really new to the unit."

"Yeah, only in-country for three weeks."

"And I think it was Charles Miller's first flight as crew chief," Greg said. "I also remember Rodney Shank, but hadn't known him that well. As for the corpsmen, I didn't really know either of them."

"One was my father, the other was Rip Tyrrell who trained Gary."

I reached in my purse and pulled out the picture of Gary and handed it to Greg. I saw the recognition in his eyes, but he didn't say a word and eventually handed the picture back to me.

"Okay, now tell me what you do," Greg said, purposely changing the subject.

"I've been doing marketing for the last several years. I began part-time in college and now I'm part of a two-person team in the communications industry. Although sometimes I feel like this research is another full-time job," I laughed. "But it's become more important than anything."

After dinner we drove Greg back to his hotel.

"I truly enjoyed meeting you both," Greg said. "I have some paperwork I'll send to you when I get home."

As we said good-bye, I debated again on whether or not to give him a hug. In the end I chickened out, although I regretted it the whole drive home.

A couple of weeks after we met, I received the reports along with a letter.

Stephanie,

I think I'm all caught up at work and home. Two weeks away is fun, but you sure pay for it when you get back.

It was very nice to meet you guys and have a few hours of conversation, and probably the high point of my NorthWest exposure. You have done quite a job of assembling a lot of varied information. The enclosed after/actions should add some more detail to the story.

I was most impressed with finding out you and your brother carry the same spirit many of us carried to Vietnam. I only wish I'd see more of it. This country needs a rebirth. It needs to go back to the values that made it great.

Semper Fi, Greg

Delighted to receive his letter, I've stayed in touch with Greg ever since. I hope to one day meet up with him again and give him that hug.

THIRTEEN

THOUSANDS UPON THOUSANDS OF PEOPLE STILL search for any semblance of closure from the Vietnam War. Attaining this measure of peace, acceptance or comfort can be elusive. Many try different approaches to bring about closure. For some, it is to never talk about their loss, hiding away all memories of those lost. For others, it comes in a trip to the Vietnam Wall or similar memorial sites.

For me, some closure came as I learned about the events that took place on the day my father died. Just discovering what happened brought peace to my soul.

Knowing Jan Bartolina also searched for what happened to her brother, I compiled all the information I uncovered into one report and mailed it to her. Jan read the report and learned all the details of the crash, finally answering all the questions that haunted her and her family for almost three decades.

This made me wonder if the families of the other four men who died with my father were in the same predicament. A man named Bill Dial played a crucial role in helping me answer that question.

To: **Stephanie Hanson**
From: **Bill Dial**
Date: **Mon, Aug 31, 1998 9:54am**

Stephanie,

I knew Gary very well. He and I were attached to the same unit. He was killed on a mission with another corpsman named Rip Tyrrell. Please call me.

I look forward to hearing from you.

Bill Dial

Using a tactic similar to police detectives, I had withheld the fact Rip Tyrrell was with my father in any of my letters or internet postings. So when I received this email, I couldn't dial Bill's number fast enough.

"I'm surprised to hear from you so quickly," he said. "I just sent the email to you less than half an hour ago."

"I couldn't wait," I responded. "I've only found a couple of people who remember Gary and I'm so excited to speak with someone who knew him well."

"I did know your father, unfortunately, not as well as I would have liked. I was his supervisor when he transferred to MAG-16 to fly medevacs. As the Administrative Corpsman, I was the one responsible for making sure those who volunteered to fly medevacs really knew the dangers and wanted to do it. I interviewed Gary several times. He was extremely eager to get flying."

"I just thought he transferred," I said. "I had no idea interviews were conducted first."

"Flying medevacs was such a dangerous job. We

needed to see if the individual could handle the stress and pressure. Gary really thought that was the ultimate in being a corpsman."

"Is there any chance that Gary flew missions at MAG-11? There have been a couple of other men who think they remember flying with Gary."

"No, Rip would not have been with Gary otherwise. We didn't like to have more than one corpsman on board. It was bad luck. Usually, except in really extraordinary circumstances, break-in corpsmen only flew one day. We lost too many people to take the chance of losing two in one crash."

He crushed any hope I had of Gary having flown more than just one mission.

"Rip Tyrrell was one of my best friends," Bill continued. "He took me under his wing when I first arrived in Vietnam. Subsequently when I took charge of flight schedules, I assigned Rip to fly with Gary on February 7th. I couldn't think of anyone better to show Gary the ropes. In fact, I drove the two of them down to the helicopter that morning."

"Was Gary really excited?"

"He was. It was a tragic loss to lose both of them in one day," Bill said. "I even wrote an article for Rip's mother a few years ago in which I mentioned Gary's name. It was an article about Rip, but I will send you copy if you like. Excerpts from the article were published in the Elmira, NY Star-Gazette on Monday, December 23, 1996."

"I would really enjoy that."

"I'll look through my paperwork and see if I can dig up any more information for you," Bill said. "And I'll get the article out to you right away."

TRUE TO HIS WORD, BILL'S PACKAGE ARRIVED JUST a couple of days later.

Dear Stephanie,

Here is the article. Hope it brings you some comfort.

I have always felt a little guilty because I didn't know Gary better. He was new to the unit and I just didn't have time to get to know him. Had he been with us longer, I have no doubt we would have been very good friends. As I say in the article, when I go to The Wall, I always speak to Gary.

I sent your name to Mary Ellen Ennis, Rip Tyrrell's sister, and told her you might contact her. We have corresponded for a long time. She seems to be a very nice lady. I think you will both benefit from talking to each other.

Hope you are well. Stay in touch.

Cheers,
Bill Dial

MEMORIES OF RIP
By Bill Dial

If you knew Rip Tyrrell you are among the truly blessed and certainly remember him: bright kid, big heart, easy to talk to. I still talk to Rip. I say hi to Gary Young too, but I talk to Rip. Gary and Rip died together, their names are very near each other on the black marble of the Vietnam Veterans Memorial, "The

Wall," here in Washington. They were killed in the crash of a Marine Corps helicopter shot down in Vietnam in '69. When I visit The Wall every year around Memorial Day I say hello to the seven other Navy corpsmen from my unit killed that year, most of them in helicopters shot down. I say hi to Gary but we don't really talk. I talk to Rip.

This year when I visit Rip, I'm going to tell him I finally got the courage to call his family. I'll laugh and tell him I'd rather fly a night medevac mission than lay out my feelings like that. Only took me twenty-six years. Talked with his mom. She was so sweet I forgot my nervousness. I should have known Rip's mom would be like that. She said Rip's dad died a few years ago. I told her how sorry I was I never told him about his son.

Mrs. Tyrrell was a little surprised to hear from someone who served with Rip. Seems most of what she knew about what happened came wrapped in the stiff prose the government uses to break bad news to families. I know because I wrote those words. That stiffness helped us hide the tears and pain we young men were not allowed to express back then. But we cried when no one was looking, drank too much and vowed to get even with the enemy.

I first met Rip when he picked me up at the First Marine Corps aircraft wing headquarters at the big air base in DaNang. I arrived in Vietnam the day before and was scared to death. I had been thoroughly brain-washed by some of the rear-area heroes in the surgeon's office at headquarters. I learned later it was some sort of initiation rite for FNGs.

"To you who is about to die, here's the one-finger salute. If the rockets and mortars don't get you, you'll die in a flaming helicopter crash."

Rip just laughed. What a pleasant change. "Not to worry," he said, "we haven't lost anyone in over a year." He made me feel at ease. I knew almost immediately I found a friend.

And friend he was. He showed me the chow-hall – important to a twenty-three year-old kid – where to get uniforms, all the stuff I needed to know. He volunteered to fly my break-in missions with me. He didn't want the hazers interfering with our primary mission, flying out to rescue badly hurt Marines, soldiers, and Vietnamese and working, often in vain, to keep them alive until we reached the hospitals around DaNang.

It is true war is a situation inflicted upon the young by their elders. The product is a young warrior that affects an image of tough ruffian, full of bluster and impervious to the horrible tools invented by those same elders solely for the purpose of tearing kids to shreds. That's the way it was, is, and always will be.

The kids who choose to care for the victims of war, the corpsmen and medics, are a little different. Their percentage of hormones varied little from their combatant counterparts. And, yes, they were armed – most carried the issue M-16 in addition to a pistol. A few tried to look like little Pattons but most were very conscious of their job – saving lives. So I had a choice, Patton or protector. Rip made the choice easy.

*Rip's calm demeanor, his easy smile, his use of
encouragement instead of denigration got me through
the scary, scary first days of my job in Vietnam. On our
first flight, we picked up a young Marine who, less
than an hour before, had both legs and an arm blown off
by a land mine. Rip told me to go for it, encouraging
me, gently suggesting ways to care for my patient. He
could have taken over or could have pushed me aside,
but he didn't. When we started taking fire from the
ground, the big machine guns opened up. The sound
terrified me, like the repeated slamming of the doors to
hell. The bullets from the ground passing through the
skin of the helicopter made little sproing noises and dots
of sky appeared where green aluminum had been before.
Rip steadied me with his gentle touch and we kept
working on the young Marine.*

*Movies about Vietnam attract me like a moth to a
flame. I know I'll hate them but I go anyway. I'll look
for every little nit-picking technical error and I always
bitch about how the troops are depicted. You never see
the Marines who built the school, or dug the well, or
held sick-call in the village for Vietnamese villagers
whom, you knew, turned right around and gave the
medicine to the enemy. But to win hearts and minds
you care for the people and heal their ailments, even
when you suspect those hearts and minds care more for
the bad guys than they do for you.*

*Twice a week Rip grabbed his bag, his box of supplies,
and with our Vietnamese nurse and one of our doctors,
went to the village down the road from our base. The
village, whose name I've forgotten, was at the base of a
natural, marble monolith appropriately called Marble*

205

Mountain. Recently, I saw a television program about former Viet Cong bases, one of which was inside the same Marble Mountain. But Rip went there willingly, sutured cuts, lanced abscesses, treated colds, removed nails, and performed dozens of other procedures to help the villagers. The same villagers who, by night, helped the enemy.

China Beach, immortalized by television, was in the backyard of our base, the Marble Mountain Marine Corps Air Facility or, simply, "Marble." We lived in metal-roofed hootches and Rip, eight other corpsmen and a Marine ambulance driver shared our hootch. Rip was the steady influence to all of us sharing our sand-encrusted, bug-infested cottage by the sea. He served as priest, surrogate parent, medical authority, and favorite nice guy. He never complained and he blew off the incessant teasing with good-natured ripostes and his charming smile.

Between Marble and the Army hospital at China Beach was an orphanage run by Roman Catholic sisters. It was a sad place. Too many children crowded its dilapidated facilities. Too many missing limbs or other horrible scars of a conflict – the politics of which they knew nothing about.

Rip frequently went to the orphanage alone, or recruited one of his buddies to come along. The sisters were not medically trained and spoke little English. Rip learned enough Vietnamese to effectively communicate. He trained the sisters, cared for the children, and worried constantly about their care. When a measles epidemic slammed the orphanage, Rip got permission to spend several days there, bathing babies to keep fevers down. He knew the danger, the nights belonged to the bad guys, but he did it anyway.

Rip died doing for someone else, Hospitalman Gary Young, what he did for me, helping Gary through those scary first medevac missions. They went in to pick up some Marines who had taken casualties from a booby-trap, a routine mission. No enemy was known to be nearby, but a big combat operation was going on and intelligence was not the best.

Back at Marble we heard the news almost immediately, the thoroughly chilling "Medevac bird is down in the zone. No activity noted." Orbiting a few hundred feet above the medevac's wingman, the "chase bird" called in the emergency. When an aircrew is in distress, all available air assets, from little spotter airplanes to supersonic fighters make themselves available to assist.

I can tell you, Walter Ripley Tyrrell, Hospital Corpsman Second Class, United States Navy is a hero. His mother can be proud of him. He represents the very best of your city, the United States Navy, and our country.

On this Memorial Day, when I talk to Rip, I'm going to tell him how proud we are.

Excited to speak to another family member and knowing it might be difficult for Mary Ellen to make first contact, I sent a letter telling her a little bit about what I discovered over the last several months and offered to share it with her family.

To: Stephanie Hanson
From: Mary Ellen Ennis
Date: Tues, Sept 08, 1998 1:08pm

Hi – this is Mary Ellen Ennis. I received your letter today. What a fascinating story! We always hoped a child of Rip's would appear at our doorstep, instead it looks like Gary's family lucked out! Did they even know you existed? It must have lightened their load to have you find them. Where do they live? Where is your birth mother? What year were you born? Do you have a great adoptive family?

I have limited memories, but the ones I do have are of a really cool brother, especially since we were nine years apart. I was a few months shy of 13 when he was killed. It was a horrible time and changed our family forever. As I get older, I miss having that big brother more and more. He would have been a great father to someone!

I would be interested in any of the info you have. It won't change things, but it kind of makes me feel closer to him.

Thanks for writing and sharing!

I sent her the same paperwork I put together for Jan Bartolina. In our subsequent exchange of emails, Mary Ellen wrote things such as, *somehow I envisioned the crash much differently* or *we always wondered why his wallet smelled like gasoline – now we know why!*

I thought how horrible that these families went almost thirty years without ever really knowing what happened. It had been only two years since I found out about my father, but to go three decades without answers seemed tragic.

Surprisingly, another family member soon added to the mix.

*To: **Stephanie Hanson***
*From: **Linda Riblet***
*Date: **Tues, Sept 15, 1998 5:48am***

My name is Linda. Rip was my baby brother. My sister Mary Ellen forwarded me all of your messages. We called him Rip because his middle name was Ripley, my paternal grandmother's maiden name. Walter was my paternal grandfather's name. RIP certainly fits his destiny: Rest In Peace. I find your situation quite fascinating.

Who were the guys who died in the crash? I used to have some of that information and I am the keeper of all of the memorabilia of Rip, but it is still difficult for me to open the boxes and examine the contents. I am having his uniform (his blues) cleaned and sealed. Rip was a very special guy. I'm not saying that because he's dead. I said it long before he joined the Navy.

Thrilled I could share my discoveries with yet another person, I immediately wrote back to Linda. The three of us continued to write back and forth, and soon Mary Ellen sent me some pictures of Rip to add to my collection – one of Rip in uniform with his mom before he left to go to Vietnam and two of Rip's name on The Wall in DC. In one picture, you could see Gary's name at the very far edge of the photo. Funny how all these years later that photo held twice as much meaning.

But my favorite picture of all showed Rip tending to Vietnamese children in a clinic, which spoke a thousand words, as I heard this was the entire essence of his being and in many ways, of all corpsmen.

I wondered if the other three families knew the details of the crash and realized I might be sitting on information that could help them. Staring at Rip's pictures, I made a vow to try to find the other families.

I FIRST SET OUT TO FIND THE FAMILY OF THE CO-pilot, Russell Moke whose mother wrote to Grandpa Del so many years ago.

I went on the internet to do a people search by typing in the name Moke and the town they had lived in. To my utter surprise, they still lived at the same address.

I picked up the phone and dialed the number.

"Hello?" an elderly lady answered.

"I'm calling for Mrs. Russell Moke," I said.

"That's me," she replied.

"Are you the mother of Russell Moke who died in Vietnam?"

"Why yes, I am."

I explained as gently as I could who I was and how I knew about her from her letter. "I've searched for the details of that day for a few years and have gathered quite a bit of information. Would you like to know a little bit more about what happened?"

"Oh, my dear, I would love it," she said excitedly. "My husband, who has since passed on, and I tried for years, but never had any luck. We didn't even get official notification from the Marines about Russ's death. They only wrote one telegram and they sent it to his wife."

"Well, I have a summary written up by some of the Marines involved and I would be more than happy to mail copies to you. I know it cleared up a lot of questions for me."

"I'm amazed you took the time to track me down," said Mrs. Moke.

"I didn't think I should keep the information to myself."

"I am grateful, dear. I've wanted to know for so many years, but gave up hope a long time ago. You know, Russell had a daughter. Marsha lives in Washington D.C., but I don't speak with her often and she doesn't talk about her dad much."

"Please feel free to give her my name and number if she expresses any interest."

"I will mention it, but I don't think she will."

"Either way is fine with me. I'll put the copies in the mail today for you."

"I'll look for it. I still can't believe you tracked me down. You are a very special young lady."

"Thank you very much. If you have any questions, please feel free to call."

I felt so good after we said good-bye and I sent the package of information to Mrs. Moke overnight.

Two weeks later I received a lovely thank-you letter from Mrs. Moke which included two pictures of Russ, peeled right out of her photo albums. One showed Russ graduating from flight school and the other in uniform prior to going to Vietnam.

Then, a few weeks later, Marsha Moke, Russ's daughter, sent me an email wanting to talk. Surprised to hear from her, I sent an immediate reply.

To: **Stephanie Hanson**
From: **Marsha Moke**
Date: **Mon, Oct 05, 1998 2:04pm**

Thanks for the response. It's really nice (and somewhat shocking) to finally meet someone who might understand what the last 30 years have been like. All this time I thought I was alone...

I was really touched by your message. Not specifically sure why, but so many things resonated with me. Learning about you came at a time when I really needed it. It's almost like a message from above. It's funny – just when I think I'm over it, I realize I'm not. And it's so comforting to know someone else can understand (although, for your sake, I wish you weren't going through this either).

My father had just turned 25 on January 19th when I was just four months old. There's this great picture of him holding me at the airport before he shipped out. Logically, I know he knew me, but sometimes that doesn't seem real. I would give anything to remember those first three months...

I, too, resemble my father in looks and mannerisms. My grandmother used to cry when she looked at me because I looked so much like my father. My mother would often comment on how I acted/reacted just like him. So, I know a part of him lives on.

"Saving Private Ryan" reminded me of Vietnam. I had no idea it would – otherwise I probably wouldn't have gone to see it. What really got me was the scene when

*they were sending the letters to relatives of the
deceased. We didn't get a letter, but a telegram. And
there were no niceties, only "we regret to inform you..."
I knew the plane had been shot down, but for many
years I thought my father died from gunshot wounds.
Only recently I learned it was from wounds to the head
sustained in the crash. I've always hoped it was fast
and painless, but have never received details on that.*

*About a month ago, I told my boyfriend the one thing I
wished for more than anything in the world was to be
able to hug my father – just once. That's what kills me
more than anything.*

*Thanks for being there, Stephanie. Thanks for helping
all of us start to heal.*

Marsha

We grew up with completely different lives, and yet
the one single wish Marsha and I would make was
identical. We would ask for just one hug from our
fathers.

LIFE GOT BUSY AGAIN, AND I PUT OFF TRYING TO
track down the remaining two families. Then an email
from Marsha changed everything.

To:	**Stephanie Hanson**
From:	**Marsha Moke**
Date:	**Tues, Nov 24, 1998 1:18pm**

I thought you might like to know my grandmother died

Sunday night. She had a stroke a few days before and never pulled out of it. She really thought you were sweet. I just keep thinking how fortunate for me that I called her on her birthday – otherwise, I may have never met you. It was the last time I talked to her and it's when she told me about you.

She was ready to leave this world. She finally found out what happened to her son and then she waited around just a little longer in order to get us together. She did her job and felt like she could go on to a better place.

Yesterday was the first time I was able to discuss my father's death with my aunt and my stepfather. In a strange way it was rather comforting – and I'd like to think you helped break the silence. It's nice to finally have him open up about it - thank you!

Marsha

The timing of it all shocked and saddened me. Realizing what procrastination could cost, I set off to find the remaining two families.

Rodney George Shank was a Lance Corporal when he died at the age of 21. He grew up in Livermore, Maine so I used a telephone directory CD-Rom to look up the name Shank in that area and found only a few.

That evening I made phone calls and after several, I reached Rodney's half-brother. I explained who I was and the purpose of my call.

"Well, I didn't really grow up with Rodney," he said. "But I would really like to see what information you have, since I don't know anything about Rodney's death."

"I can mail it out tonight," I replied. "And please don't hesitate to contact me if you have any questions."

That evening I elatedly made another set of copies for Rodney's brother.

Only one more family to find, but with the last name of Miller, I knew it would be much more difficult.

CORPORAL CHARLES WILLARD MILLER, JR. HAD been flying a little over six months at the time of his death. Only 19 when he died, he came from St. Mary's, West Virginia. Using another telephone directory list, I called all the Millers I could find for several days. After several false leads, I finally found a man whose nephew was named Charles Miller.

I once again explained the reason for calling.

"Could the Charles Miller who died with my father be your nephew?" I asked.

"Yes, that's my nephew," he replied.

I cheered silently. I had done it! I tracked down each and every family.

We spoke a little further regarding the helicopter crash. I answered a couple of his questions, but when I asked if he wanted copies of my material he hesitated.

"You know, it's just been so long. I really don't want to go through all of that again. I don't think I could read anything about Chuck."

"I completely understand, and just wanted to make the offer. Is there anyone else who might be interested?" I asked.

"No. There's no one left of the family but me."

He took down my phone number in case he ever changed his mind, but I knew he wouldn't.

Just finding all the families meant the world to me.

FOURTEEN

A LEGACY CAN BE DEFINED AS A GIFT, OR A transfer of personal property, what you leave behind, or how people remember you. When I began my journey to find out about my father, I only searched for answers. When Delbert and Steve willingly gave me all the tangible items once belonging to my father, I felt like I inherited a kingdom. Those few tokens, including his dog tags, pictures – and especially his letter tapes – were a priceless gift.

However, in the course of my journey, I discovered one more thing my father left behind for me. It turned into the greatest gift of all.

It took two events, one right after another, for me to understand. The first event started with a simple email.

To: *Stephanie Hanson*
From: *Ray Felle*
Date: *Wed, Aug 12, 1998 12:05am*

Hi Stephanie,

My wife and I just returned from Gulfport, Mississippi where we met the son of my friend who was killed in

Vietnam on 30 April 1968. I was a Corpsman in Kilo
Company and he was a Marine in my Platoon. We
were on an operation outside of Dong Ha when he got
shot in the neck. I have been looking for his family for
30 years and just found the son last November.
Meeting him was very emotional as you can well
imagine.

Ray Felle HM2 FMF 1st Platoon Kilo 3/9 3rd Mar Div
67-68

Ray's email fascinated me because his search
mirrored mine. His loyalty after thirty years impressed
me and we struck up a lasting friendship. Ray told many
stories of his time in-country, including the time when
he was in a helicopter crash himself.

To:	**Stephanie Hanson**
From:	**Ray Felle**
Date:	**Sun, Aug 16, 1998 7:56am**

We lifted off from an outpost outside Khe Sanh. There
were about 15 of us in the rear, two window 50 cal
gunners, the pilot and co-pilot. After our short trip, we
moved into the landing spot to drop off a mule (small
motorized vehicle.) The pilot aborted the landing and
circled to pick another spot.

In the process of this a parachute was blown up into the
rotors. When the two rotors came together they
exploded into a million pieces. We were about 25 feet off
the ground and came straight down on the belly of the
CH 46. The impact closed the rear door to the
chopper...the only way we knew to get on and off. Jet

fuel poured on us from the broken fuel lines and I thought I was dead. We couldn't get the rear platform doors to open. I said to myself this will be the last thing I will ever see on this earth. Then the gunners called to us from the side doors in the chopper. We all got out with only burns from the hot jet fuel and cuts from debris.

The pilots were not so lucky. The co-pilot was killed on impact when the transmission came down on him crushing him in his seat. The pilot had parts of the blade come through the window and cut his arm off at the shoulder and his leg above the knee. Someone grabbed him and put him on another chopper, but he died on the way to the hospital ship.

My understanding is that the only reason the chopper did not blow up on impact was because one of them turned the main electric switch off prior to impact. All that jet fuel running all over us! I have been trying to find an after action report on the crash.

Ray

In subsequent emails, Ray also explained how he hoped to find the families of the two pilots someday. As I kept him informed of my success, Ray turned to me for help. Although I doubted I could uncover any new information, I found it impossible to refuse.

Over the next couple of weeks, I kept my eyes open for any websites which might be of interest. One site I came upon listed various Vietnam reunions, including one for Khe Sanh veterans. Since Ray's crash occurred at Khe Sanh, I sent him the link, although I thought it probably wouldn't amount to anything. The next morning, Ray sent an ecstatic email.

> *To:* **Stephanie Hanson**
> *From:* **Ray Felle**
> *Date:* **Thurs, Sept 10, 1998 7:12am**

> *I took a moment to look at the web page and may have found the pilot and co-pilots names!!! 6/19/68 Helmstetler, Sharp. Thank you...Thank you!!!*

> *Love..Ray*

This seemed more like blind luck than anything, and I couldn't take credit for anything. I sent off a congratulatory email to Ray and returned to answering emails. I received so many emails every day, it became difficult even read them in a timely manner. One overdue email came from Bruce Lake, whom I corresponded with on a regular basis. Most of the time we just chatted about everyday events, but this time, Bruce became contemplative.

> *... I wanted to tell you a story that comes from HMM-161. A couple of real close friends of mine from flight school were killed in an incident where the blades de-synchronized.... Mike Helmstetler and Lufkin Sharp.*

> *The terrible accident happened on 6/19/68. Mike and I were really close even before we got to flight school and even pre-flight school before that.*

> *I remember standing on the helo pad in Quang Tri looking at the remains of this CH-46 and then finding*

out the pilots (who spent a minimum of 15 months training with me in all phases of flight training) were now dead. I felt sick to my stomach.

I was far, far away from home in a foreign land, in a war, learning the friends who cared most about me were now gone. I was angry, bitter, frustrated, confused, so very alone, hurt, and the list goes on and on. I didn't mean to go off on a tangent like this — maybe it's the full moon, or maybe the words just kind of came out on their own. I'd almost forgotten some of this (as I haven't dared read my own book for about eight years now for fear of the memories it will bring up).

I am afraid my recollection of events may bring tears to your eyes as they do to mine. Believe me, it's not my intent. You just continue to be a catalyst allowing me to learn what is important about my past and present. Think about it this way. For some reason I really needed to remember the loyalty and devotion and friendship of those very special men at this time, and you have helped me do that!

I pushed my chair away from my desk and stared at my monitor with wide eyes.

"No, no, no!" I said out loud.

This could *not* be happening! Bruce did *not* just tell me a story about the two men Ray wrote about that very day! The theme from "The Twilight Zone" could have started to play and I wouldn't have been surprised.

I decided to call Bruce and talk to him personally about the crash. Could this truly be the same crash?

When Bruce answered the phone, I didn't explain the

situation with Ray, but told him I needed to know more about the crash.

"I've actually got a book with a full description of the crash," he replied. "Let me find it and call you back."

After what seemed like forever, the phone rang.

"I've got the book in front of me. It's called *Masters of the Art* written by Ron Winter and has a description of the crash with Helmstetler and Sharp. Let me just read it to you."

... On June 19, 1968, helicopters from HMM-161 landed at the north end of Khe Sanh, in a place called LZ Turkey, where Marine infantrymen were gathered waiting to move out.

An aircraft piloted by Capt. Lufkin S. Sharp, with 1st Lt. Michael D. Helmstetler as co-pilot, landed and lowered its ramp.

As a squad of infantrymen ran on board, the rotor wash began whipping a parachute out of a nearby tree. Suddenly it was freed, blowing wildly in the wind, and then was drawn straight into the rotor blades. The huge sheet caught in the blades, throwing them out of synchronization. The aft rotor head tilted, then went completely out of control. Miraculously, the infantrymen and crew were not injured. But the blades smashed through the cockpit, killing Sharp and Helmstetler ...

As Bruce read this, I scrambled back on my computer and pulled up Ray's email with his description of the crash. Comparing the two, they were undeniably the same.

I didn't speak for a few moments as the truth sunk in and a dizzying mix of emotions washed over me. I finally collected my thoughts and explained it all to Bruce.

"I don't even know why I sent you that story at this time, Stephanie. I guess I felt like sharing."

"Obviously someone wanted you to tell me your story so I could help Ray. Do you mind if I give him your information?" I asked.

"Absolutely not. I might even be able to put him in touch with the families."

The moment I hung up the phone with Bruce, I called Ray. Ray had a hearing problem which made phone conversations difficult, but I couldn't wait for email.

The moment Ray answered the phone I started speaking excitedly. "Ray, it's Stephanie Hanson. I believe I've found out more information about your crash!"

"Oh Stephanie, the more I think about it, the more I don't think those were the correct names. I thought so at first when I saw it, but now I'm afraid I was wrong."

He continued talking and I finally yelled to make him hear me.

"Ray, you *weren't* wrong! It's the same crash. You *were* right about the pilot and co-pilot. They were from HMM-161 and I can put you in touch with people who knew them. There is even a book on the crash and I'll email the details to you tonight."

I had to repeat myself a couple of times, but finally Ray understood to log on to his computer.

The next morning, both Ray and Bruce wrote.

To: **Stephanie Hanson**
From: **Ray Felle**
Date: **Fri, Sept 11, 1998 7:13am**

Hi Steph,

Your call made my day and put me much closer to finding out more about the crash and the ones who died that day. We were treated so poorly as a service person when returning from Vietnam and now to find people like yourself who go out of their way to help – I don't have all the words to explain my feelings. All I can do is say a big thank you Stephanie, and to try and help others.

I wrote to Bruce Lake, Ron Winter, and also to POPASMOKE about the crash. I will keep you posted.

Love...Ray

To: **Stephanie Hanson**
From: **Bruce Lake**
Date: **Fri, Sept 11, 1998 8:49am**

Isn't it amazing I wrote about Mike and Lufkin when you had the opportunity to share it with the person who needed it? I told you in my letter it was important for me to remember those men and their dedication and all, but I didn't know exactly why. Then only a day or so later you call and explain exactly why. I'm telling you, Steph, this is all kind of "spooky." It's not just a little spooky, it's downright amazing.

A few days later, Ray wrote with the news he contacted the families of Helmstetler and Sharp. A final step in a journey he feared he would never complete.

The odds against this happening were absolutely astronomical. But what could it be other than a coincidence or fluke?

HOWEVER, A FEW WEEKS LATER ANOTHER incident happened so similar, I realized it was no fluke. One of the very first corpsmen I ever talked to, Paul "Buzz" Baviello, had been instrumental in explaining the life of a corpsman and we spoke often. One of his fellow corpsmen and best friend, Ivan Heller, also died in Vietnam and we ended up talking about it.

"So exactly how did Ivan die?" I asked.

"In a helicopter crash, just like Gary," Buzz said.

"But I thought he was a grunt corpsman."

"Yes, you're right, but he must have been flying to go on R&R or something."

"What do you mean something? Don't you know what happened?"

"Not really. I never got a straight story. Originally listed as MIA, Ivan's status changed to KIA in '73. I don't know what happened and it's bugged me for the last thirty years."

I wondered if any of my contacts could help me find out what happened, and decided to pursue it secretly until I knew more.

I sent a note off to Al Barbour, the historian at Pop A Smoke with only the information of "Ivan Heller, 2 Battalion 5th Marines Echo Company, KIA 10/11/68". I didn't think there were records on passengers, but hoped he could at least point me in a direction to search.

Within four days, I received his reply.

Steph,

Two aircraft went down that day – an H-34 and an H-46. The first eight names listed were crew members. Below is a list of all 14 KIAs, including Doc Ivan Heller, who was one of six passengers, probably all with E/2/5. The two squadrons were Marine Medium Helicopter Squadron 362 (Ugly Angels) and Marine Medium Helicopter Squadron 265 (Bonnie Sue). They were shot down near DaNang.

Al

I almost couldn't believe my luck. Bruce Lake flew with HMM-265 during the time of Ivan's death making the odds fifty-fifty he would know about the crash. I scrolled down to the list attached.

Incident Date 681011

HELLER IVAN LOUIS: HN,
  Hostile Crash Land, PAX
FERGUSON WILLIE C JR: LCPL,
  Hostile Crash Land, PAX
HALE WILLIAM THOMAS: 1stLT,
  Hostile Crash Land, Crew
HANKINS THOMAS FRED: LCPL,
  Hostile Crash Land, PAX
HARRIS LANTIE LAWRENCE JR: LCPL,
  Hostile Crash Land, Crew
HEAVER BRIAN TRACY: LCPL,
  Hostile Crash Land, PAX

HICKS BENNY JOE: CPL,
  Hostile Crash Land, PAX
KEMSKI GARY DOUGLAS: CPL,
  Hostile Crash Land, Crew
KLEINHANS LAWRENCE CHARLES: LCPL,
  Hostile Crash Land, Crew
MARTIN STEVEN WAYNE: CAPT,
  Hostile Crash Land, Aircraft Commander
RAINAUD JEFFREY WILLIAM: 1stLT,
  Hostile Crash Land, Aircraft Commander
SCHRYVER PETER EDWARD: 1stLT,
  Hostile Crash Land, Crew
WALTERS J D: CPL,
  Hostile Crash Land, PAX
WESLEY MARVIN JR: SGT,
  Hostile Crash Land, Crew

Three-quarters of the way down this list, my hands started shaking when I saw the name Jeff Rainaud, Bruce Lake's friend. I knew the story of his death well. Seeing this name meant I didn't need to do any further research. Jeff Rainaud was killed in a mid-air collision of two helicopters, so no matter which helicopter Ivan Heller was a passenger of, I knew the details of his death.

Before I called Buzz, I called Bruce to refresh my memory.

"Jeff piloted the CH-46 so Ivan must have been a passenger in the H-34," Bruce said. "There were no passengers on Jeff's aircraft. No one really knows exactly how it happened, and I heard the H-34 basically disintegrated upon impact."

"So that could be the reason for the MIA listing?" I asked.

"That's very likely. Although it technically should have been BNR, meaning Body Not Recovered. I'll email you the after-incident reports along with eyewitness interviews."

After we hung up, I emailed Buzz asking him to call me. When he called later in the evening, I tried to ease into the story.

"I know I didn't tell you, but I decided to ask my Pop A Smoke contacts about Ivan's crash," I started.

"You did? Did they even have a record of Ivan since he wasn't in the wing?"

"They had his name and I know exactly how Ivan died."

Silence filled the air.

"What do you mean you know how he died?" Buzz asked. "What did they tell you?"

"It wasn't so much what they told me, but what I already knew. They sent me a list of the men who died on the day Ivan did. There were two helicopters that went down and I recognized one of the other names on the list. Remember Bruce Lake, the pilot I told you about?"

"Yes, of course."

"His friend, Jeff Rainaud, was also killed on October 11 in a helicopter crash."

"Was Ivan in Jeff's helicopter?"

"No, but it was a mid-air collision between two aircraft. One being the helicopter Jeff flew and the other the helicopter Ivan rode in."

"A mid-air collision? I never heard anything like that about Ivan's death."

"Do you want to talk to Bruce? He's got even more details than I do and he sent me some reports to email to you."

"I don't know what to say at this moment. After all those years of wondering," said Buzz, close to tears.

"Can you send me the incident report right now before you hang up?" he asked.

"Sure," I said, and immediately forwarded the reports.

"Can you wait while I read this over?"

"Absolutely," I replied. While Buzz read over the reports, I glanced through them one more time also.

I was the crew chief on the fourth aircraft, piloted by Dick Upshaw; co-pilot Sam Kelly of HMM-265. My recollection of this incident is as follows:

While waiting our turn to land in the LZ, I heard one of the pilots say something over the IC, something like, OH MY GOD!

I immediately jumped up and looked out the windshield between the pilots and saw a large fireball directly in front of us. Initially confused as to what happened, I quickly realized our wingman hit something or was hit by something and then I saw a their CH-46 falling away. I stepped back to my door for a better view and I could clearly see the rotor blades popping off the aircraft.

I wondered for an instant if we were going to be hit by the flying debris but quickly returned to the horror of watching as they fell out of the sky and exploded in a giant fireball on the ground.

At first we didn't realize what caused this to happen but quickly came to see there was another aircraft involved. I remember speculation that it was a Republic of Vietnam

H-34 but to make matters worse, it was a Marine H-34.
These are my recollections of that sad day.

Lowell Lyman, crew chief on CH-46 in the operation.

=============================

I stood near the top of Hill 52 and watched as the CH-46
took off and began climbing out in a steep ascent with its
nose pointing south toward An Hoa. It was a clear,
sunny day with a few scattered clouds high in the sky.

At about 800-1,000 feet, the CH-46 came up
underneath a UH-34 which was flying overhead on a
similar heading. It appeared each helicopter was in the
other's blind spot and no visual contact had been made
between them.

I don't think the two fuselages actually collided but
they chewed off each other's rotor blades. An orange
fireball and black smoke erupted from the rear of the
CH-46. A series of quick clacking sounds and a muffled
explosion reached us on the ground as the blade parts
were sent flying in every direction overhead.

The two aircraft, momentarily, just hung there. Then
the CH-46, its aft end burning and smoking, began
tumbling end over end toward the ground. The UH-34
simply nosed over, the weight of the big radial engine in
its nose causing it to plunge straight down like a dart.
Thunderous noises echoed across the valley floor as the
aircraft impacted on a sandbar which extended out into
the Vu Gia River, thankfully on our side of the river, as
the other side belonged to Charlie.

The UH-34 hit first, sending up a towering eruption of bellowing fire, white smoke, and streaking shards of red flame.

The CH-46 quickly followed, close by, on the same stretch of sand. The aft section, with the engines, split away from the forward half of the aircraft in a burning heap. Black greasy smoke plumed high into the sky. The forward section did not catch fire.

The UH-34 burned white hot; so intense it was impossible to get near it. Within a few hours the wreckage was reduced to a surprisingly small mound of gray ashes, making the retrieval or identification of human remains virtually impossible. This remains one of the sadder days in my life.

Frank Powell, S-3, 3/7

When Buzz finished reading the entire email he said, "Steph, you are not going to believe this but this happened only a few hundred yards from your dad's crash."

"You've got to be kidding me!"

"Yeah, and it gets weirder. The first place I landed in a CH-46 when I got to the bush was on Hill 52. For the next month I patrolled the area where the chopper crashed and never knew. I wonder how many times I walked by it? Steph, if it weren't for you and all your dedication, I would never have known this. Thank you so much. This may sound crazy but I think Ivan and Gary must have brought us together just so you could help me."

"No, I don't think it's crazy at all. Nothing surprises

me anymore now." I replied.

"Thanks again. I think I'll go now and try to digest all of this. Hope you don't mind. Semper Fi, Steph."

CURLED UP ON MY COUCH, I STARED AT MY favorite picture of Gary from fifth grade which sat on my mantle. The silver frame engraved with stars and angels represented what he meant to me. As I sat there looking at his picture and thinking of what happened, it hit me like a ton of bricks. This was not just coincidence. This was my purpose in life.

My father loved taking care of his Marines. But he wasn't here anymore, and now it was up to me to continue his work. I had been chosen to bring these men together, to pass along the information, to listen to their untold stories, to heal whenever possible. It was what my father would have continued to do, and what I would now do.

Knowing your purpose in life is a rare and wonderful gift. After so many years of stumbling along, trying to understand what I was put on earth to do, I now knew what my father left me.

My father left me a legacy.

FIFTEEN

OF ALL THE MEDALS, AWARDS AND RIBBONS awarded in combat, for many Marines none is more valued than the Combat Aircrew Wings. These silver wings are a badge of honor for those that earn them.

Interestingly enough, corpsmen were not awarded the silver Combat Aircrew Wings, because they are listed as non-combatants under the Geneva Convention. They were awarded the gold Aircrew Wings, which are earned by Marines in peacetime. Regardless of which set my father would have been awarded, his desire to earn his wings became quite apparent, in both the letters he sent home and from some of his fellow corpsmen in Vietnam.

> *To:*   **Stephanie Hanson**
> *From:*   **Tom Eagles**
> *Date:*   **Wed, Aug 26, 1998 5:03am**

Dear Stephanie,

I met your father in the fall of 1968 at the DaNang Navy Hospital called NSA (Naval Support Activity) Hospital just across the road from MAG 16 (Marine

Air Group). I remember your father because he saw my aircrewman wings and really wanted to go flying. He felt that was the ultimate Corpsman and he asked a million questions.

I lived and worked in a village on the edge of DaNang running a Vietnamese Dispensary, treating the local populace. I always looked for help and asked your Dad to stop by. Your Dad came by a few times to help out, but he still wanted to go flying! I was sent back to the states in November, then Joe (cannot remember his last name) wrote me and told me your Dad was killed. Wish I could tell you more.

Your Dad was kind to the Vietnamese in my village – wanted to help them - gave some hours of his free time to help us hold sickcall – willing to learn - gravitated towards the kid patients – gave them money out of his own pocket to buy candy.

Have thought all day, cannot remember more, so much happened in Vietnam. I do remember your Dad wore his cover (hat) on the back of his head and my nurse, Ms. Nhan Thi Vu, thought he was so cute and handsome! She said, "Bac Si Tom ban toi Bac Si Gary Dap Chai Qua!"

Translation is "Doctor Tom, your friend Doctor Gary is very handsome!"

Wish I could say more but it has been many years.

Tom Eagles HMCM (AC) USN/RET
FMF Corpsman

In my naiveté, I assumed because my father flew one flight, he therefore got his wings, but had they ended up in the same black hole as his medals.

However, one day an email from a corpsman named John Bruneel contained upsetting information as we continued discussing how to get Gary's medals for Delbert.

> ... I would assume also Gary did not receive his AirCrew Wings? I feel Gary rates the AirCrew designation and subsequently the AirCrew Wings. Now, my feeling is certainly not the policy of the U.S. Navy. Their policy is in order to qualify for the wings, one must have earned one air medal, flown five combat missions or 11 regular missions. Under this policy, of course, Gary would not have earned his 'wings.'

Reading these words felt like being hit with a jackhammer. Like learning Gary only flew one mission, learning he hadn't earned his cherished wings was a bitter pill to swallow. John valiantly tried to console me when he learned of my mistake.

> Stephanie, whether Gary flew 1, 3 or 500 mission takes nothing away from his status (in my eyes and many other people's) of hero. He voluntarily put himself in Harm's Way, when he could have sat back in a not so dangerous job and probably got home safely.

Although I took his words to heart, I could not shake off the heartbreak I felt over this. Those wings represented the fulfillment of my father's dream and the loss of them haunted me.

I THINK JOHN FELT RESPONSIBLE FOR BREAKING the news about the wings to me, for he spent a lot of his time trying to help get the other medals and ribbons my father earned.

Finally, after several months of endless letter writing, I received a large envelope from the National Personnel Records Center. I ripped it open and a found a full copy of Gary's military records which they finally located.

I pored over these records from beginning to end, from his Enlistment Contract down to the last order reassigning him to MAG-16. Although I didn't understand all the terminology, I gathered some new information. Gary enlisted for Aviation Duty, Medical Service Duty and Dental Service Duty, in that order. He wanted to fly from the very beginning. February 15, 1968 was the day he volunteered for duty in the Republic of Vietnam and in September of the same year, he went to Vietnam and got assigned to MAG-11. The formal records showed his transfer to MAG-16 on February 5, 1969, just two days before he died.

But, the most exciting discovery was a copy of the citation and certificate for the other medal Delbert talked about.

The President of the United States takes pride in
presenting the AIR MEDAL
(Bronze Star for the First Award)
posthumously to

HOSPITALMAN GARY NORMAN YOUNG
UNITED STATES NAVY

for service as set forth in the following:
"For heroic achievement in aerial flight while serving

as a Corpsman with Maine Air Base Squadron Sixteen, Marine Aircraft Group Sixteen, First Marine Aircraft Wing in connection with operations against the enemy in the Republic of Vietnam. On 7 February 1969, Hospitalman Young launched aboard a CH-46 transport helicopter assigned a medical evacuation mission southwest of DaNang in Quang Nam Province. Arriving over the designated area, the aircraft immediately came under intense enemy fire and sustained several hits. During the approach to the landing zone, he was mortally wounded when the CH-46 crashed as a result of the heavy volume of hostile ground fire. Hospitalman Young's courage, bold initiative and selfless devotion to duty earned the respect and admiration of all who served with him and were in keeping with the highest traditions of the Marine Corps and of the United States Naval Service. He gallantly gave his life in the service of this country."

I had heard of the fairly prestigious Bronze Star medal, but having some questions on the posthumous awarding, I sent John an email.

To:	*Stephanie Hanson*
From:	*John Bruneel*
Date:	*Wed, Oct 07, 1998 2:27pm*

Stephanie,

I received your quick note from last evening. To answer your question, it would be really hard to tell without seeing the citation. If you have a copy of it please fax it to me. Gary may well have earned it (Bronze Star) for services prior to his shoot-down (even at MAG-11).

*More important. You said the record says he was
awarded the Bronze Star. Do you know if it was ever
presented to his parents? The reason I ask is that early
on in our conversations, you mentioned his dad had a
couple of medals. By my count, he should have received
at least four:*

1. Bronze Star
2. Purple Heart
3. Vietnam Service
4. Vietnam Campaign

Your friend
John

This message puzzled me since John was a very
astute man and in my email to him, I clearly told him the
citation stated for actions the day Gary died, and not for
any prior actions. But I must not have been as clear as I
thought, and wrote him another email clarifying this.

After I wrote to John, I decided to also fax him a copy
of the citation, just for kicks.

To:	**Stephanie Hanson**
From:	**John Bruneel**
Date:	**Wed, Oct 07, 1998 6:46pm**

Dear Stephanie,

*Received the fax, and of course the email. Guess this old
brain can still figure out some of the techno stuff.
Regarding the award. It is NOT the Bronze Star.
Please look at the first line. "The President of the
United States takes pride in presenting the AIR*

MEDAL (Bronze Star for the First Award)
posthumously to:"

This award is for the "AIR MEDAL." A little
explanation: When a medal is awarded to an individual
more than once, the military has to have a way of
showing it is a 2nd, 3rd, 10th or even 25th award of the
same medal. With some awards they may show it as a
"palm cluster." On others (most) it is a star. A tiny
bronze star is then attached to the medal to signify how
many awards of that medal have been given.

Now the important part of the award is contained in the
first five words of the CITATION: "For heroic
achievement in aerial flight." Why is this important?
For a couple of reasons.

1) The AIR MEDAL was given for different reasons.
One could earn it simply by flying five combat missions
(simply is a gross understatement in this context) or it
could be issued for one heroic achievement. Gary's was
for heroic achievement – the key word here is 'heroic.'
He was not simply a man doing his job – he was and is
a genuine HERO.

2) If I understand what I've been told – an award of the
AIR MEDAL qualifies an individual for designation as
an aircrewman and the subsequent award of the
Aircrew Wings. If I am right in this Stephanie, Gary is
not only deserving of his Aircrew Wings, he was
entitled to them.

So now, my dear friend, here is what I know. Gary
ABSOLUTELY rates the following awards.

1) AIR MEDAL (w/bronze star)
2) PURPLE HEART
3) VIETNAM SERVICE MEDAL
4) VIETNAM CAMPAIGN MEDAL

And more likely than not – Aircrew Wings.

There were also a couple others awarded by the Vietnamese government, he might possibly rate – but I don't have a clue how to verify these.

VIETNAMESE CROSS OF GALLANTRY w/palm
VIETNAMES CIVIL ACTION w/palm

Now these last two were given to just about everybody who served there (at specific times).

OK, what should we do about it? What do you want to do? I think (my opinion only – you and Gary's family have to do what you have to do) you should petition the Navy for these awards. I will do everything (in my limited power) to help you if that is what you want. These awards are the mark of the man Gary was. They should never be taken lightly and should be passed on to his heirs. Let me know – I really don't know where to start, but will start at your request. There are more than a couple of channels open to you – Congressman/Senator, Navy personnel, Marine Corps personnel – I WILL HELP IN ANY WAY I CAN. It doesn't make a difference who they are eventually given to – just as long as they are given. Will close for tonight. You take care and KEEP THE FAITH.

Love, John

For a split second, I felt like a complete idiot having thought the citation was for the Bronze Star. I took a look at my copy and sure enough, it said Air Medal. I guess the words Bronze Star just stood out because of familiarity.

My feelings of idiocy were quickly forgotten as the enormity of what John wrote sunk in. If the information John received was correct, my father earned his wings!

The question was what to do about it. It intimidated me to write a Senator for something like this, as surely it wouldn't be important enough for them to get involved. I thought my best bet would still be with the Navy, so I did some further research and found a Navy Liaison office who reportedly helped veterans in obtaining their medals. Once again, I wrote a letter requesting my father's medals and ribbons, only this time I enclosed a copy of the Air Medal certificate.

In the meantime, I joyously wrote and updated everyone I knew about my latest discovery. Once again, Rich Kiselewsky came forward with information that would change everything.

To: **Stephanie Hanson**
From: **Rich Kiselewsky**
Date: **Thurs, Oct 08, 1998 1:49pm**

Dear Steph,

Keeping in mind this was a long time ago and I'm leaning on the old side of life now, I remember it as this.

Air Crew Wings were indeed prized. As to Air Medals, I recall it took a specific number off missions to earn one OR after a "significant" mission a person could have received a "single mission" air medal.

240

Indeed Gary may be entitled to Air Crew Wings.
It is possible that while it was his first day of flying, he
may have flown more than one mission for the day.
Each landing at different grid coordinates counted as a
mission. Hence, you could fly one day and fly many
"missions."

You might check and see if anyone still has his flight
records for that sad day. Such records may show how
many missions they flew.

Also, the Marine Corps may have a record of the
missions the aircraft and crew flew on the day of your
Dad's passing. Again, the best people to contact are the
Navy and or Marine Corps, but don't forget the good
people at Pop a Smoke. They still have "connections" in
the Marines and may be able to shake a tree or two to
get things on the move so you can receive your Dad's
wings.

Sorry I can't be of much help on this one for you but
good luck in your new quest and let me know how you
make out. If the information I gave you is in error
please don't hold it against me – remember – I'm
OLD!!! I'm sure I speak for all the men of 364 when I
say ... Gary EARNED his wings!!!

As always, Rich

My hopes soared at Rich's email. Could Gary have
flown more than one mission? The flight records would
be taken from a pilot's log book, but would my luck
hold out that Jan Bartolina still had Ernie's logs? I
crossed my fingers and sent off an email.

To: **Stephanie Hanson**
From: **Jan Bartolina**
Date: **Thurs, Oct 08, 1998 7:24pm**

Yes, we do have one of his flight logs – at least the last one. It's at my mom's. Would it help?

Jan

The one book I needed. Jan promised to make copies that weekend and fax them to me.

After an interminably long weekend, I received Jan's fax on Monday morning. The log pages listed flights for both January and February, but I couldn't decipher the majority of the codes and numbers. I needed to get a helicopter pilot to help me interpret it all, so I faxed a copy to Bruce Lake.

He called me in the afternoon and we went through the entries one by one. Laid out in several columns, Bruce explained what each one stood for.

1st column – The day of month the flight took place on. There were two pages, one for January and one for February.

2nd column – The model of helicopter flown. All of Ernie's flights were in a CH-46D.

3rd column – The serial number of the helicopter. The serial number of the helicopter flown for that day was 153334.

4th column – Flight Codes. There were various codes listed throughout Ernie's log, but on

February 7th, it listed 1R6. The coding is as follows:

1 = Daylight Visual

R = Service Flight

6 = Medical Evacuation into/out of enemy fire area

If the entries were written in red ink, it meant they took fire on the landing, and the missions were counted twice. All the flights in February were marked in red.

5th column – Total flight time. 2.7 hours for February 7th.

6th, 7th, and 8th columns – Flight hours as pilot, co-pilot or A/C Commander. Ernie flew 1.4 hours as pilot and Russ Moke flew 1.3 hours as pilot. Since Russ was still fairly new to the unit, Ernie served as A/C Commander for the entire 2.7 hours.

9th column – Sea/Land landings. The number of total missions flown that day.

As I heard the explanation for the last column, the number on the paper swam in front of my eyes. This column was marked with a seven. Not one, but *seven*. Gary flew seven missions that day before the final fatal one. Gary earned his wings and fulfilled both of his dreams.

Now it was up to me to get them acknowledged.

DIGGING THROUGH ALL THE PAPERWORK I KEPT on this process, I came across the suggestion from John

Bruneel to contact a Congressman. At this point, I would write to anyone. Of Oregon's two Senators, I decided to write the senior Senator and spent two days composing a letter. Although afraid my request might not be important enough, I felt hopeful the minute I dropped the letter in the mail.

But several months went by without an answer. Stumped as to what to do next, I truly felt I failed my father.

Then one day I stumbled upon a television show called "Suicide Missions – Medic."

Towards the end of the show, Senator Max Cleland from Georgia came on. I hadn't heard of him before and listened intently as they told his story of service in Vietnam. Senator Cleland served in the Army during Vietnam. On one of his missions, a grenade explosion severely wounded him and he ended up losing both legs and one arm. Unexpectedly, there happened to be four Navy corpsmen on the next hill. They heard the explosion and rushed to help and saved Senator Cleland's life.

At the end of the program, Senator Cleland stated, "I hope every medic in the military – regardless of what branch they serve in – realizes they have one United States Senator one of their predecessors saved on the battlefield who appreciates their service."

The statement stayed with me all night long and in the morning I decided to write Senator Cleland. Perhaps the fact my father was a corpsman would at least get someone to read my letter. If it got ignored, I would be no worse off than before.

And after six months went by, I believed Senator Cleland's office had ignored my letter. Then, in October of 1999, I unlocked my mailbox to find a very large package jammed into it. I tugged it out and saw there was no postage on it. How could something get through our postal system with no postage? I looked to the return address, which simply stated *Senator Max Cleland*. Could it be? Were my father's medals actually in this envelope?

I ran to my apartment, threw my bags and purse on the floor, and tore open the envelope. Two letters and four boxes fell out. Before I opened the boxes, I unfolded the two letters.

October 12, 1999

Dear Ms. Hanson:

Enclosed are the medals and awards the Bureau of Naval Personnel reports your father, Gary Norman Young, earned. Please accept them along with the thanks of a grateful nation.

I appreciate the opportunity to help make the system work as it was intended. Thank you for your patience and perseverance.

> *Most respectfully,*
> *Max Cleland*
> *United States Senator*

Tears welled up in my eyes when I saw the personal signature of Senator Cleland. To know an out-of-state Senator went to bat with the military for my father's medals touched my heart.

The second letter came from the Bureau of Naval Personnel, Retired Records Section.

Honorable Max Cleland
ATTN: Simon Gaskill

This is in response to your request on behalf of GARY NORMAN YOUNG concerning military awards.

A review of Military Records shows the veteran is entitled to the enclosed awards:

PURPLE HEART MEDAL

AIR MEDAL – WITH 1 BRONZE STAR

VIETNAM SERVICE MEDAL – WITH 2 BRONZE STARS

REPUBLIC OF VIETNAM CAMPAIGN MEDAL – FOREIGN

REPUBLIC OF VIETNAM MUC GALLANTRY CROSS – FOREIGN

NATIONAL DEFENSE SERVICE MEDAL

If further information or assistance is required, please feel free to contact this office directly.

Sincerely,
C.E. SMITH
LT JG, USN

My father earned six medals. Only four boxes were enclosed, but a postscript explained how to obtain the two foreign medals, since they were not issued by the

United States Government, but by the Vietnamese Government. Two of the boxes were cardboard, while the other two were leather-bound cases. I opened the two cardboard boxes first. They contained the Vietnam Service Medal and the National Defense Service Medal, including the corresponding ribbons.

Smiling, I opened the other two cases. There in front of me were my father's Purple Heart Medal and the Air Medal mounted on velvet lining. The Purple Heart gleamed with its purple and gold colors and the Air Medal was royal blue and gold, with an eagle embossed in flight.

I'm sure my father would have downplayed their importance, as did all the other servicemen about the medals they themselves earned. But finally having official acknowledgement was very important to me.

Suddenly, I realized I hadn't seen anything on the Aircrew Wings. I searched the envelope again, but to no avail. Although grateful to have the medals for Steve and Delbert, I needed to get the wings for my father.

The next day I called Senator Cleland's office and asked to speak with Simon Gaskill, whose name appeared on the letters. When he came on the line, I introduced myself and thanked him for all of their help in getting my father his medals.

"I do appreciate the medals more than you'll ever know, but I also wanted to see if you found out anything on the Aircrew Wings," I explained.

"No, I couldn't find out how to get those issued," he said. "I did ask a few people, but no one has ever been involved in a request like that."

Although bitterly disappointed, I didn't push the issue, for I was truly grateful for the medals.

THAT WEEKEND I DROVE OUT TO DELBERT'S house.

We visited for a while before I began leading up to the subject.

"Grandpa Del, I've worked on something for a few years in regards to Gary. I know how upset you were when you didn't get all of Gary's medals and I decided a while back to try to get them for you."

"You did? All this time?"

"I wanted to keep it a surprise for you. I thought I could get them with no problem, but it turned out to be much more difficult than I thought."

I reached down into my bag and pulled out the package from Senator Cleland.

"I finally found a Senator who helped me. It even took him several months, but he sent these to us last week."

Delbert opened the envelope and pulled out the contents. I showed him each medal individually, saving the best for last. Finally I picked up the Air Medal case and opened it.

"This is the Air Medal that Gary earned," I said gently.

Putting the medal gently in his hands, the look on his face made every moment of hair-pulling frustration I encountered worthwhile.

SIXTEEN

VETERAN'S DAY OF 1998 WAS THE FIRST TIME I SAW my father's name on The Wall in Washington, D.C. since discovering the truth. Having thought a million times about my original trip to The Wall in 1992, I felt both excited and nervous to see it again.

I technically visited The Wall on the day before Veteran's Day, knowing it would be less crowded than on the official holiday. The taxi driver dropped me off on Constitution Avenue that cold and gray morning, but thankfully the rain had stopped. I walked to the path which wound its way along the top of The Wall. Although I couldn't see it, I could still feel its presence directly below me. My hands shook so I sat down on a park bench to collect my thoughts. After weeks of anticipation, I wasn't ready to face the names on The Wall. Not just my father's name, but now all the other names I knew. The men who flew with my father, the buddies my friends lost, the brothers and fathers of people I knew. The list went on and on. So much more than a list of names, this was hallowed ground to me.

The Wall has only been in existence since 1982 and in a city with hundreds of years of history, it is fairly new in comparison. It is where people go to grieve over those who were lost, and yet no one is buried there. But this place, in many ways, holds more importance than the actual graves of the 58,249 names.

Walls are typically built to divide and keep people out. This wall is the only wall ever built to bring people together. And bring people together it does. It is listed as the most visited outdoor memorial in the nation, with over two and a half million visitors each year.

These visitors leave something of themselves behind. Some items left, such as dog tags, medals, ribbons and pictures are self-explanatory. But other items fall outside of society norms. Items that have no monetary value and no outwardly symbolic value, such as beer cans, cigarettes and playing cards, but to someone, they hold great meaning. Every item has a story behind it. There is guilt in many of the items left and perhaps by leaving the items for those who never returned, people feel some semblance of peace.

The majority of the items left are just plain letters. Some left open for the public to read, or just scratches on bits of paper, while others are formally typed and sealed. I planned to leave a letter also, but hadn't quite finished composing it in my mind yet. Twice a day, volunteers collect the items left behind and take them to a special warehouse to be categorized and stored. My letter would end up in that warehouse and possibly someday in a display for all to see, so I wanted to make it perfect.

Getting chilly sitting on the bench, I finally stood up and walked towards the entrance to The Wall. Still not quite ready to see it, I walked over to the bronze statue called *The Three Servicemen* and stared at it for quite some time. Because of the sporadic rain throughout the morning, the raindrops made it appear as if the men were crying.

On one of my past trips to The Wall a soldier had pointed out the realism of the statue, down to the dog tag laced into the laces of a boot of one of the soldiers. He told me how the men sometimes wore one around their neck and one on the boot because of the destruction the mines caused if stepped on. This way there were two chances for identification of the body.

A group of school children crowded around me in an effort to get closer to the statue and I moved several steps away. This distance gave me a new perspective on the statue, as the men appeared to be looking at something. They all faced in the same direction with the same solemn look on their faces. I turned slowly until I saw what they were looking at. The soldiers silently guarded their fallen brothers.

I looked back at the statue of the three men. They seemed to say, "Go ahead, Stephanie. Go down to The Wall. We'll watch over you."

With newfound courage, I took a deep breath and began walking towards The Wall. Reaching the top of the sloping path, I looked for Panel 33W, Row 83. The Wall lists the names of the lost in the order they were taken from us. The list actually begins at the apex of The Wall starting with the date 1959. The names go out to the end of the East Wall, which appears to recede into the earth, and then resumes at the opposite end on the West Wall as it emerges from the earth. I entered at the West Wall with the first panel, Panel 70W. The Wall grew taller and taller as I ventured further down the path. The numbers located at the bottom of the panels grew smaller. It felt like a countdown of the time remaining until I would find my father. 40, 39, 38 ... Finally I stood directly in front of Panel 33W. Somewhere on this panel was my father's name. But before I looked for Row 83, I turned around and got my bearings. In shock I realized this was where I broke down in tears back in 1992. *Right here* I first knew my father was on The Wall. Spooky seemed an understatement.

Finally I turned and faced The Wall again. From pictures people sent me of Gary's name, I knew it was a few rows up from the bottom. The Wall is made of black granite and polished to a mirror-like surface to reflect the surrounding images. However, when it rains, the names and marble turn a grayish-white, and it is very difficult to read the names. I tried reading the bottom few lines but had trouble deciphering the names. The National Park Service has volunteers at The Wall at all times to answer questions and help visitors locate names, but I needed to do this alone. I purposely didn't ask anyone to come with me to The Wall, nor did I arrange to meet any of the veterans for a few more hours. I had to do this by myself.

So I next tried using the dots on the side of the panel to find Gary's name. In addition to the panel numbers, there are 1,170 dots to help find a name. The dots are etched at every tenth line, however, with the height of the panel and the diminished clarity of the names, it was impossible for me to see to the top to find the first few dots. After several minutes, I wanted to panic. I couldn't read any of the names and yet I knew my father's name was right in front of me. I turned around resigned, thinking I would have to summon a Yellow Cap volunteer for help. But I didn't see one in close proximity and I didn't want to move away from the panel. I glanced back at The Wall and my eyes caught a name I knew. Ernest Bartolina. My heart filled with joy the moment I saw it. The individual names on the panels are also in chronological order; within each day, the casualties or missing are listed in alphabetical order. I scanned through the names for the next few rows until I saw the name. *Gary N. Young.* I sat on my heels and touched my father's name.

"Hi Dad," I whispered softly. "It's me, your kid."

This scene reminded me of a painting called "Reflections" by Lee Teter. This memorial print shows a man in a business suit leaning against The Wall in sorrow. Inside The Wall, his fallen comrades reach up and place their hands to his. I know it's mythical, but thinking of Gary being on the other side of this Wall comforted me. With a lump in my throat I quietly spoke to my father this way for several more minutes.

I then located the names of the other men who were killed with him. Ernie Bartolina, Russ Moke, Chuck Miller, Rodney Shank and Rip Tyrrell. I touched each name reverently and passed along messages from the family members I knew. I lingered over Rip's name, thinking of all he did for Gary knowing I would never forget the price he paid for training my father.

I had a couple of hours left until I met with Jim Schueckler and Julie Kink, and I needed to visit other names before then. Many veterans had asked me to look up names and pass along messages and I took this very seriously.

After completing all my visits, I walked back to Gary's panel. As I stood there, out of the corner of my eye I saw a Yellow Cap volunteer helping a couple to the right of me. Glancing at his nametag I saw the name Jim Schueckler.

When he finished, I walked up to him.

"Hello, Uncle Polecat."

He didn't even ask my name and wrapped his arms

around me in a great big hug. It seemed so right we met for the first time in front of Gary's panel.

We visited for quite a while and then he asked, "Would you like to make a rubbing of Gary's name?"

"Would you do it for me?"

Having Jim create the rubbing would be of great significance to me. The veteran who started it all had truly earned this honor.

When it was complete, Jim handed it to me and I carefully put it in my bag.

"How about if we do rubbings of all six of the men who died together and leave them here?" he asked.

Jim made another rubbing of Gary's name and I pointed out the others. When all six were complete, we propped them up at the base of The Wall, to be linked together forever.

Shortly after we finished this project, Julie Kink found us. With hugs all around, it felt like a family reunion. We talked for a while and even joked at times.

The first time we burst out in quiet laughter, I immediately felt guilty and irreverent. This should be a place of quiet and reverence. Looking around to see if the veterans and other visitors looked at us in disgust, I saw while many people had tears in their eyes, there were also plenty of others smiling and laughing like us. Yes, this was a memorial for those we lost, but also so much more, a place for connections and people to come together, whether in grief or happiness or both. Somewhere, men like my father and Julie's brother, were together watching us meet for the first time and probably bragging how it was all their idea in the first place.

We walked around for hours and they introduced me to many veterans. In their minds, my father made the ultimate sacrifice and they gave me the respect and admiration he earned. I was accepted completely and without question.

I didn't talk too much in those next few hours, but sat back and listened to their stories. With some of them, it was like opening the floodgates, once they started talking, they didn't stop. But I didn't mind as I could tell many of them had waited for years for someone outside of their veteran friends to show an interest in their time in Vietnam.

Eventually I headed back to 33W, where I would meet Marsha Moke. Even though we didn't know what the other looked like, we knew we would find each other. The Wall had finally dried out making the marble reflective again and I glanced at The Wall and saw a reflection of a girl walking towards me. Our eyes caught and she walked right up to me without hesitation and we threw our arms around each other.

We finally pulled apart and I laughed. "Boy, I sure hope you are Marsha!"

"I am," she assured me. "I don't know how, but I just knew it was you!"

She had lots of questions about the crash and I pointed out the other men who were on the helicopter. She promised to always include them in her future visits to The Wall.

I pulled the album of information I compiled out of my bag and Marsha flipped through the pages.

Quietly Marsha said, "I do have one question I've been anxious and scared to ask. The one thing I need to know is ... did my father suffer?"

"No, he didn't. I have it on very good faith none of them suffered. The crash was sudden and painless for the men."

Marsha's eyes filled up with tears. "I've been looking for that answer for almost thirty years. I needed to know and here you come along with the answer. I can't tell you how much peace it brings me. A huge burden has been lifted off my shoulders."

Marsha asked me to pass along a message to Greg Tomaro and all the veterans who helped me along the way.

"Please tell the vets they have the power to pass on our fathers' hugs."

A COUPLE OF DAYS LATER, I MET UP WITH BRUCE and Kay Lake to visit The Wall again. When we arrived I took them right to Gary's panel.

The night before I finally got what I wanted to say down on paper, which I now pulled out of my pocket. Bruce thoughtfully purchased a rose for me to leave and, using it as an anchor, I left the letter for my father propped up at the base of his panel for all to read.

For Gary N. Young, Corpsman
KIA 2-7-69

Dear Dad,

Hi. You never knew me, but now I know you do. Thank you for all you've given me. The strength to be a survivor. The courage to get to know you. The determination to continue my search. And THANK YOU for my smile. It was once yours and now it's mine. That crooked grin you always seemed to wear.

I know how much you wanted to fly and get your

*wings. I discovered you flew 2.7 hours that day of
flying. I hope you had the time of your life. You flew 7
missions which means you EARNED your wings. I
don't think you knew that. I am getting you your
wings. They WILL be awarded, even though it is almost
30 years later. I will wear them for you with pride as I
do with your dog tags. Thank you for what you did. I
love you.*

Your little girl,
Stephanie

Bruce and Kay sensed I needed some time alone and they wandered off to find other names. I walked a few feet away from the panel and waited to see the response to my letter. I wasn't sure if anyone would stop to read it, but if they did I wanted to be there to see their reaction. Quite a few people stopped to read my letter, some bent over to move the rose so they could read the final lines and then respectfully put the rose back in place.

One such man I will never forget, although I don't know exactly why. He walked along The Wall with another friend, both dressed in nice business suits. It didn't appear he was looking for a name, just at some of the items left behind. He walked over to my letter and read it once and then read it again.

He called out to his friend, "Hey, Felix, you have to come read this letter."

That is all I heard. I have no idea exactly what touched me so, but perhaps because he seemed to care so much for two people he didn't know. Watching both of them read my letter with tears in their eyes is a memory I will never forget.

When Bruce and Kay rejoined me, Bruce placed his own letter to Gary behind mine.

An open letter to Gary N. Young
Nov. 3, 1948 to Feb. 7, 1969

Dear Gary,

We never had the chance to meet each other, but I know we saw each other at work. Only recently, I learned you were a Corpsman in Vietnam. I am certain there were dozens of times you heard the rotors of my helicopter overhead and you began running to the helicopter landing pad near DaNang to assist the wounded men being carried off our aircraft on stretchers or even poncho liners. We never even looked at each other as you were already treating the men we were both working so hard to save and I was leaving for another rescue mission. And, there must have been times in the field when you treated some of the injured Marines who were being brought to my helicopter, so I could rush them to the nearest medical facility or to the hospital ship off the coast of Vietnam. We worked on the same team, you and I, and I would have been honored to know you.

How very sad for all of us that in our efforts to save others, you were taken from us.

I never had the chance to thank you for the men you treated and the lives you helped save ... some of whom were my best friends. I never had the chance to shake your hand or to give you the hug you deserve ... and neither did your daughter.

*Let me tell you about your daughter, since you never
had the opportunity to meet her. She has worked hard
to learn all she can about you. She has learned that
many people have such special memories of times spent
with you. She shares this information with us and now
I feel I did know you. I can tell you your kindness and
joy of life lives on in your daughter. Just as you left so
many fond memories in the minds of others … she does
the same. By continuing her search and caring the way
she does, she shows us some people really do care about
veterans and what we did in that awful war. Just as
you worked so hard to treat those with physical
injuries, your daughter has helped so many of us with
unhappy memories…. memories that continue to haunt
and bother us to this day. She helps by giving us the
courage to face our fears and get on with life. You
would be so very proud of her Gary! Even though you
cannot be here with us, your memory will continue to
live on through your daughter, Stephanie, and the
knowledge and strength she shares with us.*

*I know this is long overdue, Gary, but I just wanted to
let you know I am proud to have had the honor to work
with you and I thank you for all you have given us.*

*Sincerely,
Bruce R. Lake
1st Lt. USMC*

Later that afternoon, we finally left and hailed a taxi
to follow up on Bruce's idea to go to the Navy Yard and
see if the Archives held any new information on the
helicopter crash. Once there, we asked for the
declassified information on HMM-364 for the month of

February. I didn't know if they would give me any information but the clerk handed me a box full of unit diaries. It was so easy, I almost couldn't believe it. We searched through the paperwork to find the sections for February of 1969, of which the clerk made copies.

PART III
SIGNIFICANT EVENTS

3. *CASUALTIES FOR THE MONTH*

NAME – RANK – SERNO - SERVICE - KIA/WIA

BARTOLINA, E. E. – Capt – 094529 – USMCR – KIA

MOKE, R. E. – 1stLt – 0100517 – USMCR – KIA

MILLER, C. W. – Cpl – 2291066 – USMC – KIA

SHANK, R. G. – LCpl – 2290575 – USMC – KIA

TOMARO, G. J. – Cpl – 2263491 – USMC – WIA

4. *INTELLIGENCE*

7 February 1969

HMM-364 flew 71 sorties for 30.0 flight hours, lifting 3.0 tons of cargo and 98 troops/passengers. Fourteen Med Evac missions carried 9 Emergency, 21 Priority and 1 Routine evacuees while expending 2250 rounds of .50 caliber ordnance in support of the following Operation and Units: Taylor Common, 1ˢᵗ MARDIV, MAG-16 and HMM-364. Four fire incidents were

*reported with (YK-14) being shot down with 6 KIA and
1 WIA. (YK-11) received 2 rounds of enemy fire, (YK-
12 7/8) and (YK-3) received one per aircraft from
enemy fire.*

YK-14 was my father's helicopter. All the information I struggled to find right at my fingertips. Had I received this paperwork in the very beginning, I would have known instantly Greg Tomaro was the survivor, among other things. But, I also knew it wouldn't have meant as much. They all would have just been names on a piece of paper, but now I knew them for the men they were.

SEVENTEEN

SINCE 1988, THE POP A SMOKE ORGANIZATION holds a reunion every two years, for men to get together with the men they suffered and sacrificed with.

I first heard of Pop A Smoke, just a couple of months before their 1998 reunion in Pensacola, Florida. Since I couldn't attend that reunion, I anxiously looked forward to the 2000 reunion in San Diego. At the beginning of each reunion year, the Pop A Smoke website shows a daily countdown and I watched the counter every day, until it finally said *0 days and a wakeup* and I headed to San Diego.

With 5,000-plus active members at the time, Pop A Smoke expected a couple thousand people to attend the reunion. Although I knew a couple of Purple Foxes who would be there, most of the men I corresponded with would not. This meant the great majority of the attendees would be strangers, and although I was speaking at the Purple Fox dinner, I wasn't positive everyone would believe I belonged at the reunion.

After checking into the hotel, I set off to find the Purple Foxes. The organization hosted functions which encompassed all squadrons, but for the rest of the time most of the members hung out with their individual squadrons.

I reached the Purple Fox Hospitality Suite and walked into the main living room. At the far end of the room, I could see a group of men in the kitchen and deck area, sitting around talking and laughing. I froze for a minute, too scared to approach the group, then forced myself to walk over to the table.

They all stopped talking and looked up at me without saying a word.

"Hi, I'm Stephanie Hanson."

Before I could continue, the man closest to me jumped up and gave me a big hug.

"Stephanie, it's me, Daryl Riersgard!"

Relief flooded over me and I started to laugh. Daryl and I wrote several emails back and forth during my search. I couldn't have asked for a better person to introduce me to everyone. I sat down and within minutes was answering questions and talking with everyone as if I had known them all my life.

From this point on, everyone welcomed me with open arms. The reunion became one of the most amazing experiences of my life. Everywhere I turned, I saw men, talk, laugh and sometimes cry as they discussed their experiences from Vietnam. All around, you could sense the healing taking place.

ON FRIDAY NIGHT, EVERYONE SPLIT UP TO ATTEND their individual squadron's dinner. I went to the Purple Foxes dinner at the Officer's Club at Miramar Air Base, where I was scheduled to give a speech. I worked for months writing and practicing on anyone I could get to listen, as I wanted to deliver it without breaking into tears.

Being my first speech, I was so nervous I don't

remember much until "Uncle" Frank Gulledge, one of the squadron coordinators, introduced me. As I walked to the podium, I tried not to let anyone see how much my hands shook, placed my notes in front of me, looked around the crowded room, took a deep breath and began.

For those of you who might not be familiar with my story, I'll give a quick background first. I was adopted at birth by two very wonderful people. We never knew anything about my birth parents, but that was okay with me. However in 1996, I was forced to search for my birth parents due to medical reasons.

I soon located my birth mother and after a shaky beginning, we now have a great relationship. She was the one who told me about my father - Gary Norman Young. He was a Navy corpsman and he volunteered to serve over in Vietnam. After he left my mother discovered she was pregnant, but decided not to tell Gary in a letter. She planned on meeting him on his R&R, but he was killed three weeks prior to this, never knowing he was about to have a child. He was only 20 years old.

Two months later, I was born. Alone, overcome with grief, and only 21 herself, my birth mother made the painful decision to give her baby up for adoption. She and Gary were not married and she felt a family could provide the child she carried a better chance at life than she could as a single mother.

The only thing my mother had left in regards to my father was his obituary from our local newspaper. It stated he was killed in a helicopter accident while on a recovery mission, but that wasn't enough information for me. I needed to know more about both my father and exactly what had happened to him.

I decided to try my luck on the internet. Not too long after that, I located what was left of Gary's family – his father and his younger brother. They were absolutely thrilled to have a part of Gary left in this world and welcomed me with open arms. From them, I was able to learn more about my father and who he had been, but it turned out even they didn't really know much more about how he died or about his time in Vietnam. They did have a box of Gary's possessions, which they gave to me. Going through the box was like starting to put together the pieces of a puzzle. I could soon put together a timeline of his tour in country from the letters he sent back to his family.

Gary went to Vietnam in September of 1968 and was stationed at the dispensary in DaNang. But what he really wanted to do was fly. Getting his wings became his main goal. He tried for five months to get transferred to a helicopter unit, but it wasn't until the last week of January in 1969 that he got sent to MAG-16. He was so excited knowing he would soon be flying! On February 7th, he finally got his wish and began flying medevac missions. But one day was all he got. He was killed on just his 8th mission.

Learning this little bit of information only made me want to know more, so back to the internet I went. For almost two years, I kept searching with no success. Then I was finally pointed to the website of Pop A Smoke. I began to send out inquiry letters to a few of the members, not sure of what I was doing or if I was going to offend anyone with my search. I was very nervous about the whole thing. But from the very start, I received responses from some wonderful people who encouraged me to keep doing what I was doing and declared I would eventually discover what I was looking for, if I just kept at it. So I kept writing – hundreds of letters actually. In the beginning, I really didn't think I would get much response. I knew the chances of finding someone who knew my father from the short period of seven days at MAG-16 were slim and why would anyone answer if they hadn't known my father? But to my complete astonishment, the responses came pouring in. And in and in. To date, I have received almost 1,000 emails, letters and phone calls. It's been overwhelming and surpassed my wildest hopes.

In my mind, I categorize the responses into three different groups. Many of you in this room fall into one of these categories.

The first group is the veterans who didn't know anything about my father or his accident. You were either from different squadrons or weren't even in Vietnam at the same time as my father. These were the letters that surprised me the most, I think. I wouldn't have expected you to bother writing me back, but you did in enormous numbers. And while you may not have known my father, you helped me out more than you can imagine. What you did was teach me both about Vietnam and also just how Corpsmen fit into the picture.

It made me recall when I first told my brother Geoff about my birth father. Geoff served in the Marines for

*four years in the early 90s even going over to Saudi
Arabia during the Gulf War. I thought he would be
excited to hear my father also served in a war. Before I
showed him the newspaper clipping, I said, "My dad
was in the service too. He was in the Navy." At this,
Geoff just rolled his eyes and said, "Oh Stephanie, did
he have to be a Squid?" But he took the newspaper
clipping from my hand and when he was finished
reading it, he looked up at me and said, "Your dad was
a Corpsman, Stephanie. He wasn't a Squid, he was a
Marine." Now, four years later, I truly understand
what he meant.*

*I was so ignorant about all of this but I now had the
best teachers in the world – those who were there. The
words written about Corpsmen were so touching and
poignant. I had no idea how highly-thought of
Corpsmen were by the Marines. It took these letters for
me to understand just how special that relationship is.*

*The second group consists of veterans who didn't know
my father or much about the accident, but what you did
know were the men who died with my father. There
were many of you that wrote to me with stories,
pictures and anecdotes about the other five
crewmembers. It made me think there might be others
out there in the same situation as me – looking for
answers. I spent many months tracking down the
families of the other crewmembers and shared with
them all the wonderful things said about their loved
ones.*

*There are many, many people this information has
brought great comfort to. I want you to know the*

families and friends of Ernie Bartolina, Russ Moke, Chuck Miller, Rodney Shank and Rip Tyrrell will be forever grateful and send their thanks to you.

The last group is the small number of veterans who knew my father and were with the Purple Foxes the day of my father's death. Even though I know just how difficult it has been to bring up the memories of such an awful day, you still came through for me.

From Jim Bandish – a crewmember on the wingman chopper, Greg Tomaro – the lone survivor of my father's crash, the members of Courtney Payne's recovery team and those back at Marble Mountain that day either in the ready room listening to it all or dealing with the aftermath, I have been able to piece together exactly what happened before, during and after the medevac mission. I've learned how many men risked their lives to try and rescue those lost, even when they knew it was hopeless, emphasizing the age-old tradition that combat Marines never leave behind wounded comrades, and attempt to recover their dead as well. I've learned what a great loss this was to the Purple Foxes and MAG-16. In addition to losing four members of your squadron, you lost two Docs in one day, which was absolutely devastating. I know it wasn't easy for any of you to talk about it, but the fact that you did this for me, means more than I can ever say.

I have learned what great fortune it was for me for my father to have been flying with the Purple Foxes that day. Many men from other squadrons expressed their admiration of your unit. You are a very respected and highly regarded group and I've been told many times

268

other Marines longed to have been with your unit. One of the highest honors I've ever had came the day Col. Brady personally welcomed me as a member of the Purple Fox family.

One of Gary's greatest sources of pride was in "taking care of his Marines." He mentioned this over and over in his letters. To quote him from one of his tapes....

"Marines over here treat the corpsmen just great, 'cause the way they figure it, if anything happens to us, you know, who's going to take care of them? But seriously, they really respect the rate of the corpsmen, it's unbelievable. It really makes us feel good and we do as much as we can for them too."

I know how happy Gary is sitting up there watching all of his Marines now take care of his little girl.

To be so openly accepted by all of you has been one of the best experiences of my life. While I can never get my father back, I have many new family members now. I have certainly been adopted once again by so many of you. You have helped more than I will ever be able to express. So right now, the best way I know how is to just say "thank you" and "welcome home."

When I finished my speech, I looked up at the crowd and saw them all staring back at me in silence. The moment seemed to last forever, and for a moment I wondered if I had said something wrong. Then every person in the room stood and a thunderous ovation broke out. Many in the audience cried and several people took my picture. During the applause, I finally felt like I gave something back to all the men who gave me a part of themselves.

With my speech over, I relaxed and spent much of the rest of the time comfortably hanging out on the suite's porch with the Purple Foxes.

On the last day, Richard Bianchino, a pilot with HMM-364 in 1969, pulled up a chair next to mine.

"Stephanie, I figured out a way to get your wings," he exclaimed. "It came to me at three o'clock this morning. I think the problem is you aimed too high in writing to the Senators, Marine Corps and Navy. Wings were typically issued by the Commanding Officers. There wasn't any official paperwork, and so the people you talked to would understandably not know how to get these awarded."

"Okay," I said. "What should I do?"

"You need to start at the bottom. The Purple Foxes are an active-duty unit down at Camp Pendleton. We need to write to their Commanding Officer and put your request in through him. I'll help you pull together all the information you need, if you like."

I became hopeful again hearing this different angle. The moment I got home, I once more gathered all the supporting data. Richard and I compiled a formal request and I sent the package off to the current Commanding Officer of HMM-364.

I knew it would take time for my request to go through the proper channels, and wasn't really concerned as the months rolled by and I received no response. The local media picked up on my story and a newspaper article and a television news segment came out on my journey. This brought forth more people who knew my father during his childhood and high school years, and I joyously met with all of them.

Once things calmed down, I realized almost a year had passed since writing to the Purple Foxes Commanding Officer. I checked with Richard and learned a change of command had occurred and there was a new Commanding Officer at HMM-364. We decided to resend my information, and I dropped another packet in the mail on September 10, 2001.

The day before September 11.

That morning, I knew my request would go to the bottom of the pile, and rightly so. We, as a nation, had more important things to take care of in our time of sorrow.

FINALLY, ON FEBRUARY 7, 2002, THE ANNIVERSARY of my father's death, I decided to try again. But due to current affair of the world, it was extremely difficult to get mail through to our military and I wasn't sure how to best approach HMM-364's Commanding Officer.

Every day I visited the Vietnam Purple Fox website Frank Gulledge created, where people posted notes daily on the bulletin board. One frequent visitor was Master Gunny Sergeant James "Top Bix" Bixler, an active-duty Purple Fox and the only active member who had served in Vietnam.

On a whim, I decided to write Sergeant Bixler to see if he could give me any tips on how to get my information into the proper hands. He sent me a quick reply, stating he would see what he could do, and to my great surprise, the answer arrived in less than two weeks.

To: **Stephanie Hanson**
From: **Marvel Capt Justin E**
Date: **Tues, Feb 26, 2002 5:51pm**

Ma'am-

My name is Captain Justin Marvel and I am the Adjutant for the Purple Foxes. LtCol Scott has made it a priority to do whatever we can to get combat aircrew wings awarded to your father. To that end after making some calls to HQMC, I think we have a lead on how to get this process started.

The information we'll need will be the following:

1) Did your father complete a locally administered course of instruction and get assigned as a crewmember? (It should be in his record book if you have a copy of that.)

2) Do you have a certificate from the Commanding Officer of that time designating him as a naval aircrewman?

3) Do you have any flight log books or documentation to the effect of his being an aircrewman?

From what I have been able to gather I think we stand a pretty good chance of getting this done. Any information or documentation you have would definitely help. Please write me back at your earliest convenience, as we are deploying to Korea on the 5th of March for a few months and I might not be able to get e-mail while I'm there. I look forward to hearing from you.

Justin Marvel, Captain, USMC
Adjutant, HMM-364
"The Purple Foxes"

After years of getting absolutely nowhere, I finally believed this was the right track. Since Captain Marvel's questions were more attuned to the Marine Corps and not a Navy Corpsman, I consulted with Richard Bianchino and other medevac corpsmen I knew, and we determined what paperwork should suffice as proof.

- *Gary's records assigning him to MAG-16*
- *The Air Medal citation stating killed in combat while serving as a crewmember*
- *Ernie Bartolina's logbook*
- *Letters from Bill Dial and Gene Brady*

I put all my faith in Captain Marvel and yes, that is his real name. He certainly lived up to this moniker. Even after several months of deployment to Korea, Captain Marvel stayed on course, and just a few weeks after the unit's return stateside, he contacted me again.

To: **Stephanie Hanson**
From: **Marvel Capt Justin E**
Date: **Wed, Jun 19, 2002 4:09pm**

Ma'am-
I have heard back from HQMC and it sounds like what we have is enough to get the wings and get them entered in his official record. I will keep you informed as to what the timeline is in getting things squared away and awarded. I am going on leave till the 8th of July, but when I get back, hopefully we'll know more. But it's looking good so far.

- Capt Marvel

I tried desperately not to get my hopes up with this email, but I will admit for the first time I felt my father's wings were within in my grasp. And several weeks later, I knew the outcome.

To: **Stephanie Hanson**
From: **Marvel Capt Justin E**
Date: **Fri, Aug 2, 2002 10:59pm**

Ma'am-

We have achieved victory!!!!! Please let me know how you would like to have this presented. I'm sure we could work it out for a ceremony either up in your neck of the woods or down here at the squadron. I will also let the "Purple Fox" Vietnam alumni know. Congratulations, my only regret is that it took so long to get.

- Capt Marvel

The tears flowed freely as I read this email. After four years of work, my father finally would get his wings.

Captain Marvel refuses to take credit for making this happen and I know many Purple Foxes and several others at Marine Corps Headquarters all worked on this project, for which I will always be grateful. But I also know Captain Marvel put many personal hours into this and since we've continued to stay in touch and I've subsequently met him, I know he will absolutely hate me for saying this, but Captain Justin E. Marvel is my personal hero.

He sent me the official message from Major "Dirt" Hayes, who also deserves a great deal of credit.

To: **Scott Col Michael W**
From: **Hayes Maj Kent W**
Cc: **Marvel Capt Justin E**
Sent: **Thurs, Aug 01, 2002 4:11 AM**

Sir,

I am pleased to tell you the Combat Aircrew Designation (posthumously) for Hospitalman Young was signed yesterday afternoon. I am sending the original designation letter via FEDEX this AM. Have Capt Marvel give me a call and I will fax an advanced copy as well.

If there is anything else we can do for the "Purple Foxes," let me know!

Semper Fi, Dirt

Major Kent W. "Dirt" Hayes
Headquarters, U. S. Marine Corps
Aviation Manpower Support Branch

The thought of a ceremony hadn't even crossed my mind, but the timing turned out to be perfect. The next Pop A Smoke reunion was being held in Pensacola, Florida in a few months. I wrote to Frank Gulledge and asked if I could have just a couple of minutes for Gene Brady to present the wings to me at the squadron dinner. I thought it fitting for Gene to be the presenter, being the Purple Fox Commanding Officer the day my father died.

My request was met with great enthusiasm from all involved in planning the dinner and I forwarded this information on to Justin, hoping it could work out.

To: **Stephanie Hanson**
From: **Marvel Capt Justin E**
Date: **Fri, Aug 2, 2002 10:59pm**

Ma'am-

I've informed Col Scott as to your wishes and he agrees it would be fantastic to award the wings in Pensacola. We'll figure out the details as to how to get them to the reunion. On behalf of today's Purple Foxes I can truly say it has been an honor and the highlight of my time in the Corps to help in some small way to get those wings. We never forget men like your father. The legacy he helped pass on to us is fiercely cherished... I never met him, but I can say myself and many others here think of him every day. I will keep you informed as to what plans develop and whatever your wishes are, we will get them done.

- Capt Marvel

EIGHTEEN

MY JOURNEY CAME FULL CIRCLE AT THE 2002 POP a Smoke reunion.

I arrived in Pensacola in the midst of Hurricane Lili, but even the strong winds and rain couldn't dampen my excitement. I expected everyone to be happy for me, but the level of excitement over it all took a mysterious turn. Whenever I mentioned the ceremony, the men would just smile like the cat that ate a canary and walk away. Their behavior puzzled me, until I finally got Frank Gulledge to spill the beans.

"Well, Stephanie, the Commandant of the Marine Corps heard the story about your father's wings," he said cheerfully.

This statement left me speechless.

"He tried to change his schedule around so he could fly down to Pensacola and award the wings himself to you," Frank continued. "But, unfortunately he couldn't make it. So instead he is personally sending a three-star General down to do the honors."

I covered my mouth with my hand and slowly sank into a chair.

"*The* Commandant? The head of the Marine Corps? A three-star General?" I finally managed to stammer.

"Yup, it's turned into quite a big deal," he chuckled.

No greater honor could have been given to my father and having the Commandant personally involved went beyond my wildest dreams.

As soon as possible, I pulled out my cell phone and called my brother.

"Hi, Geoff. Umm, you'll never guess what happened. Somehow the Commandant heard about the wings."

"You're kidding!"

"Nope. And because he couldn't come down to Pensacola himself, he is sending a three-star General down to award them."

After a moment of silent, he replied, "Holy shit, Stephanie!"

"I know!"

"I don't think I ever even saw a three-star in my career. Let alone, be in a room with him or speak to one," Geoff said in awe.

Hearing those words underlined what an incredible honor this was, not just for my father, but also for all the Purple Foxes. How did I get so lucky?

THE NEXT NIGHT WE ARRIVED AT THE MUSTIN Beach Officer's Club. Typically we did not have a head table at the squadron dinners, thereby keeping all of the attendees at the same level of honor. With so many different Commanding Officers of HMM-364 throughout the unit's years in Vietnam, it wasn't appropriate to choose one over another to sit at a head table. But when I walked into our room, I saw a long table up on a stage at the far end of the room.

And of course, they put me up there along with Gene and Ginny Brady, Major General Michael Hough,

General Jack Woodmansee, Jan Bartolina, and Larry Kachelhofer who was a member of the local press.

"Why, why, why ... " I mumbled nervously.

Several Foxes who stood within earshot laughed. "*Obviously* we need a head table with a three-star General attending," one of them explained.

"But why do *I* have to sit up there? I just want to sit with all you guys," I nearly wailed.

The group laughed again. It was fine and dandy for them to laugh, since they weren't the ones who had to get up in front of nearly 200 people and talk! This was more nerve-racking than the speech in San Diego, because I had nothing prepared, nothing written out.

Major General Hough arrived before the dinner and we all took our seats.

John Harris, a Purple Fox pilot in 1969, began the ceremony by introducing the General as the keynote speaker. In due course, I learned John was the one responsible for getting my story in front of the Commandant.

I have the privilege of introducing a good friend of mine. He's wearing two stars and has been nominated and confirmed for three stars, the President just has to sign the piece of paper and he gets to pin them on. He is the head of all Marine Aviation, he owns Marine Air. He's what we call now the Deputy Commandant for Aviation. The Marine Corps was classy enough to send somebody down and he was classy enough to be the guy to come down to help us do this for Stephanie and for her father, Gary Young.

Mike enlisted in the Navy – he was a squid. In 1963, he was smart enough to get accepted into the Naval

Academy, graduated from the Naval Academy in 1969, went to Basic School, then came down here to Pensacola for training. His sole goal in life was to fly CH-46s, but he didn't pass the test! (This sarcastic comment brought roaring laughter.) So they gave him his second choice – fighters – and he flew F-4s and F-18s. He did the normal things you do to make General Officer, high-level staff, high-level command. The pinnacle of his career was MAG-24 where he had the Purple Foxes as one of his resident squadrons. So he did get to go down and fly 46s with the Purple Foxes and he lived through it. He looks pretty good for it – lost a little bit of hair ... but not bad.

So, ladies and gentlemen, it is my pleasure to introduce Major General Michael Hough.

General Hough walked over to the podium and began his speech, combining just the right amount of seriousness and humor to make his speech one of the best I have heard.

This is a hell of a deal. First of all, I'm back with guys my age! I saw the nameplates out there, and I saw the numbers, and I said "man, they are almost 69-70 years old. Jesus, your wives look good!"

You know it's interesting, when I walked in the door, you can always tell an outfit by what happens, and you just feel the tempo, seize the moment. The first thing I saw was Walt "The Worm" and Sherm "The Pig" and some other real cuties that came up to me and said, "Hey, how's it going" and I thought, "I don't have a clue who these guys are!"

But the point is, let me tell you what really happened. I could tell as soon as I walked in this room, the air was electric, it was ecstatic for a lot of reasons. Number one, I could tell you all wanted to be here. Number two, I know there is a center-figure here. I know you are all called Brady's Bunch, and I was honored to meet your leader here, and there is an absolute reason why he is the centerpiece in your lives. I also know why you all stood up for him. Although, I could tell you what I told him – man, you must have pictures on all these guys. (Once more, the room broke into laughter.)

But to all the young people, the sons, the daughters that came here with your dads, I will tell you the reason they're all here is because it is a priority in their lives. When you do a hard thing together, it glues you up, it binds you up, and as a matter-of-fact, you really find out what it's all about early in life.

This is a night of heroes. I've been doing a lot of things throughout my life, I've been to a lot of functions, in fact, far too many functions. But these are the kinds of functions that are the best. You've come here because you want to be here, you've come from all over the United States, and the reason you're here is to celebrate the fact that you're all on the vertical, but also by virtue of the fact, you are amongst heroes. You are truly amongst heroes, and from where I sit, you are all heroes.

And tonight is a spectacular night, a one-of-a-kind, one I have never experienced in my life, where not only am I amongst heroes, heroes of the past, heroes of today, but what you're going to do tonight, on behalf of this young

lady sitting next to me, is a spectacular occasion. A
spectacular occasion, where something is going to be
righted after so many years. And it wasn't done simply
because of accident. It happened because of men and
women like you out here, because of your leader, and
also because the Marine Corps felt this was absolutely
very important. Truly she is a role model herself, a girl
following in her dad's footsteps. Why? Because of her
persistence. Her persistence to find out what happened
and then to make it happen.

And for that, what I would like to do is tell each and
every one of you that it is an absolute honor for me to be
here. On behalf of the Commandant of the Marine
Corps, it's an honor to be here to represent what he
thought was so important. He would have liked to have
been here himself tonight but he had a conflict – he's in
a meeting with the President.

But the reason I want to tell you what was so
important in this celebration, it's not only a celebration
of what you have done for your country in war, but
because of the corpsmen of this country, the Navy
Corpsmen who have so oftentimes been the real heroes
on the battlefield. The ones who get so often, not the
credit, but the ones that are always by our side who are
often unarmed, and so forth, who have suffered the
extremes to the max, the dangers of the battlefield, and
yet they are still hospital corpsmen, the ones who have
devoted their lives to nothing more than saving
Marines lives.

I don't know how many times I've passed the Annex,
where maybe some of you have worked in Washington,

*D.C., where it's corpsman after corpsman after
corpsman with the Medal of Honor – so deserving.*

*Tonight, what you're going to do is celebrate one of
your own. Truly, one of your own. One that you served
with, and one sadly that died on the battlefield, far too
young. However, in his honor, we've got his daughter.
And tonight, this is not my show, but yours. It's yours,
and your leader, Gene Brady, who is going to present to
the daughter, a set of Aircrew Wings, ones her father so
richly deserved and earned years before.*

*So this is a very, very special occasion, a tremendous
night and it's an honor to be here. I ask each and every
one of you to take care of yourselves, and more
importantly, you take care of each other.*

Thank you very much.

During the standing ovation for General Hough,
Gene Brady stepped up to the podium.

*It's an honor to have you here tonight, General Hough,
and congratulations on that third star.*

*Gary did not know he was a father-to-be, when he went
overseas. Stephanie was adopted, and because of
medical reasons, years later when she was checking on
her biological father and mother, she came upon the
story of the Purple Foxes. She had an insatiable appetite
to find out everything about her biological father, and
she began her search and she ended up with the Purple
Foxes. That's a story from several years ago, and we
adopted her. She became almost paranoid about getting*

his Aircrew Wings and she persisted – you can't get rid of her! Nor do we want to! But she searched everywhere, the Headquarters of the Marine Corps, the Chief of Naval Operations, everywhere ... but she finally got with one of our heroes, Richard Bianchino, and he gave her directions. He said "start at the bottom." Rich gave the direction, she took her marching orders and she went.

So, we have our Purple Foxes, still an active squadron down in Camp Pendleton. We started there with my successor, LtCol. Mike Scott. We have an adjutant there, named Captain Marvel, who is truly a marvel ... he gets in touch with an active-duty Major at Headquarters of the Marine Corps, appropriately named "Dirt" Hayes. Here we are some thirty-three years later and it was a question of whether he really rated the Wings because there are certain requisites – one being so many missions. But what we found out was that he flew on a multi-number mission, so every one counted as a mission. That qualified him, but it was hell, going back through the squadron diaries. Finally they came through and Mike Scott's adjutant delivered the wings to me last week and I was almost in tears. The emphasis is that the active-duty guys are just so fantastic ... here you are, a three-star general coming down to see us ... it's amazing.

I'd also like to acknowledge two men here with us today. If we could get Bill Beebe and Dr. Clay Linkous to stand up, please. These two men were on the recovery team for Stephanie's father and Jan's brother.

And now we're going to cut right to the heart of it.

Ernie Cunningham will read the citation that after thirty-three years has arrived. I have the wings to present to Stephanie and I hope the General will join with me in the presentation.

Before they read the citations, Gene beckoned me to stand between him and General Hough. Ernie Cunningham stepped up and read the two citations prepared for my father, neither of which I had seen.

From:	*Commandant of Marine Corps*
To:	*Commanding Officer*
	Marine Medium Helicopter Squadron 364
Via:	*(1) Commanding Officer*
	Third Marine Aircraft Wing
	(2) Commanding Officer
	Marine Aircraft Group-39
Subj:	*Combat Aircrew Insignia*
	Eligibility ICO
	Gary Norman Young, USN
Ref:	*Combat Aircrew Request*
	Capt Marvel, fax dtd 19 June 02

1. After careful consideration of the records contained in Ref (a), this department has determined that your request for initial awarding of Combat Aircrew Wings (posthumously) for Gary Norman Young/USN is hereby authorized.

2. The Marine Corps further recognizes Hospitalman G. N. Young's devotion to duty and his sacrifice to country. The designation of Combat Aircrew cannot begin to express our deepest appreciation.

3. This authorization is permanent and it is recommended you forward this authorization to the Chief of Naval Personnel for appropriate entry into Hospitalman Young's official records.

D.L. Barraclough
Head, Aviation Manpower & Support Branch
Aviation Department

=================================

From: **Commanding Officer**
           Marine Medium Helicopter Squadron 364
To: **Stephanie Hanson**
Via: **Commanding Officer**
           Marine Medium Helicopter Squadron 364
           (Feb 1969 – Aug 1969)
Subj: **Combat Aircrew Insignia**
           Eligibility ICO
           Gary Norman Young, USN

1. The history of HMM-364 clearly shows a unit that will stand "shoulder-to-shoulder" and if necessary, "back-to-back" while effectively serving and preserving the interests of our nation. This dedication and an ability to work as a team is fueled in part by a love for our country and our esprit d'corps, a key part of what makes us Marines. While serving as a member of the Purple Foxes, HN Young epitomized the best of these qualities and without a doubt, HMM-364's exemplary reputation today is a tribute to the sacrifice of heroic Marines and Sailors, like HN Young, who were the ultimate patriots. By his courage and unfaltering devotion to duty in the face of grave personal danger

*and through his selfless sacrifice to his country, HN
Gary Norman Young upheld the highest traditions of
the Marine Corps and the United States Naval Service.*

*2. It is with great honor and personal pride that I
deliver the initial awarding of Combat Aircrew Wings
(posthumously) for Hospitalman Gary Norman Young.*

M.W. Scott

At this, Gene reached into the podium and pulled out
the wings. But he did not hand me a set of the gold
Aircrew Wings.

My father received the coveted silver Combat
Aircrew Wings.

In addition, the active-duty Purple Foxes had
mounted them in a shadow box on a piece of
camouflage material, with purple matting representing
the Foxes, and brown leather representing a flight jacket.
Underneath the wings a black plaque with gold letters
stated:

*HN Gary N. Young, USN
In recognition of his selfless sacrifice to his country*

*Feb 7, 1969 Quang Nam
" ... lest we forget ... "*

I struggled to keep my composure at this
presentation.

Gene Brady then called Dr. Clay Linkous up where
he presented me with a set of miniature wings. This set
was for me.

Gene then nodded giving me the go ahead to speak. I

used to make fun of people who accepted awards or gave speeches and later said they couldn't remember a word. Well, the joke was on me this time, for only when I saw a videotape of the ceremony, did I know what I said.

> *My dad really wanted these wings. I made a promise to him four years ago I would get them, and I can't thank you guys enough for helping me.*

> *On his enlistment records, he put down he wanted to do aviation and then medical service. Those were his top two choices. He loved being a corpsman, but I know that one day he added flying to being a corpsman was just the greatest thrill for him.*

> *It means a lot for me to be able to share this with all of you. So many of you have helped me get here. Especially Rich Bianchino, for putting me on the right path. It's an honor to have Gene Brady participate in this – he truly is my Papa Fox. And it's an honor to have the General here – thank you.*

> *It means a lot to share this with you guys, because you know these are not just wings, but a badge of honor. And for that, I thank you and Semper Fi.*

To thundering applause, I took my seat. Jack Woodmansee nudged me and said, "Pin the miniature wings on."

"Oh, no," I protested. "This is not my honor; these are my father's wings."

Jack reached over and tapped General Hough on the shoulder. "Will you pin the wings on Stephanie? She won't do it herself."

I could only watch as General Hough picked up the miniature wings and pinned them on my sweater.

"There, you *will* wear this set of wings," he said.

"Yes, sir," was all I could manage to say. I wasn't about to argue with a three-star General.

Leaning back in my seat, it felt like a fairy tale with a flawless script. Everything had fallen perfectly into place. The promise I made to my father four years earlier was fulfilled. The kindness of strangers turned a small ceremony into an extraordinary honor for him. His wings were presented in a room full of heroes.

And I knew my father watched with a big crooked grin on his face.

ABOUT THE AUTHOR

Originally from Portland, Oregon, Stephanie Hanson Caisse now lives in Mississippi with her husband. SgtMaj Rick Caisse retired from the Marine Corps after 30 years and now continues his service to our country as a MCJROTC instructor. Stephanie provides marketing for small businesses in various industries and continues to help veterans with their journeys. Her story has been featured in several newspaper and magazine articles and an Emmy Award-winning TV segment.

Visit her online at www.acorpsmanslegacy.com.

CPSIA information can be obtained at www.ICGtesting.com
Printed in the USA
BVOW09s1922301014

373050BV00014B/213/P